Contents

Alma Triangle Shawl 2	Granny Square Dish Towel 33
Granny Square Jacket 6	Iconic Granny Couch Afghan 35
Bobby Granny Square Blanket 10	Granny Square Scarf & Earflap Hat ... 38
Gramercy Granny Scarf 13	Granny Square Dog Sweater 41
Urban Granny Dog Sweater 15	Multi-Granny Square Market Bag 43
Diagonal Granny Afghan 17	Granny Square Sweater 46
Bellona Granny Shawl 20	Granny Triangle Scarf 50
Corner Granny Blanket.................... 22	Sparkly Granny Hat......................... 53
Granny Motif Market Bag 25	Silvery Granny Throw 56
Granny Afghan/Shawl..................... 28	Granny Square Market Bag.............. 60
Granny Square Dish Cloth 31	Vintage Hues Granny Afghan 62

6

15

28

35

43

53

Alma Triangle Shawl

Easy

MEASUREMENTS
Finished Width (top edge) Approx 72"/183cm
Finished Length (at center) Approx 36"/91.5cm

MATERIALS
YARN
LION BRAND® Feels Like Heaven, 3½oz/100g balls, each approx 246yd/225m (nylon)
- 2 balls in #141 Mauve (A)
- 2 balls in #100 White (B)
- 3 balls in #153 Charcoal (C)

HOOK
- Size size I-9 (5.5mm) crochet hook, *or size to obtain gauge*

NOTIONS
- Tapestry needle

GAUGE
1 Granny Square = approx 6½"/16.5cm square and approx 9"/23cm across diagonal.
BE SURE TO CHECK YOUR GAUGE.

NOTES
1) 28 Squares and 8 Triangles are worked separately, then sewn together following Layout Diagram to make the Shawl.
2) Trim is worked all the way around outside edge of assembled Shawl.
3) Squares are worked in joined rounds. Triangles are worked in rows.
4) Yarn color is changed every 2 rounds/row following Color Sequences. To change yarn color, fasten off old color and join new color as instructed.

COLOR SEQUENCES
COLOR SEQUENCE I
Work 2 rnds with A, 2 rnds with B, and 2 rnds with C.

COLOR SEQUENCE II
Work 2 rnds with B, 2 rnds with C, and 2 rnds with A.

Color Sequence III
Work 2 rnds with C, 2 rnds with A, and 2 rnds with B.

Color Sequence IV
Work 2 rows with B, 2 rows with C, and 2 rows with A.

SHAWL
GRANNY SQUARES
Make 28 squares in total: 12 following Color Sequence I, 7 following Color Sequence II, and 9 Squares following Color Sequence III.

With first color of color sequence, ch 4; join with sl st in first ch to form a ring.
Rnd 1 (RS) Ch 4 (counts as dc, ch 1), [3 dc in ring, ch 1] 3 times, 2 dc in ring; join with loose sl st in beg ch-4 sp—you will have four 3-dc groups and 4 ch-1 sps in this rnd.
Rnd 2 Ch 4 (counts as dc, ch 1), 3 dc in same ch-sp as joining sl st, *ch 1, (3 dc, ch 1, 3 dc) in next ch-1 sp (corner made); rep from * 2 more times, ch 1, work 2 more dc in first ch-sp; join with loose sl st in beg ch-4 sp (first corner completed)—eight 3-dc groups and 8 ch-1 sps.
Fasten off.
Rnd 3 From RS, draw up a loop of 2nd color of color sequence in any corner ch-1 sp, ch 4 (counts as dc, ch 1), 3 dc in same ch-1 sp, *ch 1, 3 dc in next ch-1 sp, ch 1, (3 dc, ch 1, 3 dc) in next corner ch-1 sp; rep from * 2 more times, ch 1, 3 dc in next ch-1 sp, ch 1, work 2 more dc in first ch-sp; join with loose sl st in beg ch-4 sp—twelve

3-dc groups and 12 ch-1 sps (three 3-dc groups and 2 ch-1 sps along each of 4 sides between corner ch-1 sps).

Rnd 4 Ch 4 (counts as dc, ch 1), 3 dc in same ch-sp as joining sl st, * [ch 1, 3 dc in next ch-1 sp] twice, ch 1, (3 dc, ch 1, 3 dc) in next corner ch-1 sp; rep from * 2 more times, [ch 1, 3 dc in next ch-1 sp] twice, ch 1, work 2 more dc in first ch-sp; join with loose sl st in beg ch-4 sp—sixteen 3-dc groups and 16 ch-1 sps (four 3-dc groups and 3 ch-1 sps along each of 4 sides between corner ch-1 sps). Fasten off.

Rnd 5 From RS, draw up a loop of 3rd color of color sequence in any corner ch-1 sp, ch 4 (counts as dc, ch 1), 3 dc in same corner ch-1 sp, *[ch 1, 3 dc in next ch-1 sp] 3 times, ch 1, (3 dc, ch 1, 3 dc) in next corner ch-1 sp; rep from * 2 more times, [ch 1, 3 dc in next ch-1 sp] 3 times, ch 1, work 2 more dc in first ch-sp; join with loose sl st in beg ch-4 sp—twenty 3-dc groups and 20 ch-1 sps (five 3-dc groups and 4 ch-1 sps along each of 4 sides between corner ch-1 sps).

Rnd 6 Ch 4 (counts as dc, ch 1), 3 dc in same ch-sp as joining sl st, *[ch 1, 3 dc in next ch-1 sp] 4 times, ch 1, (3 dc, ch 1, 3 dc) in next corner ch-1 sp; rep from * 2 more times, [ch 1, 3 dc in next ch-1 sp] 4 times, ch 1, work 2 more dc in first ch-sp; join with loose sl st in beg ch-4 sp—twenty-four 3-dc groups and 24 ch-1 sps (five 3-dc groups and 4 ch-1 sps along each of 4 sides between corner ch-1 sps). Fasten off.

TRIANGLES

Make 8 following Color Sequence IV.

Row 1 (WS) With first color of color sequence, ch 6, (3 dc, ch 1, 3 dc, ch 1, tr) in 6th ch from hook (5 skipped ch at beg of row count as tr, ch 1)—Two 3-dc groups, 3 ch-1 sps, and 2 tr.

Row 2 Ch 5 (counts as tr, ch 1), turn, 3 dc in first ch-1 sp, ch 1, (3 dc, ch 1, 3 dc) in next ch-1 sp (corner made), ch 1, (3 dc, ch 1, tr) in beg ch-sp—four 3-dc groups, 5 ch-1 sps, and 2 tr. Fasten off.

Row 3 (WS) Draw up a loop of 2nd color of color sequence in first tr, ch 5 (counts as tr, ch 1), [3 dc in next ch-1 sp, ch 1] twice, (3 dc, ch 1, 3 dc) in corner ch-1 sp,

Alma Triangle Shawl

ch 1, 3 dc in next ch-1 sp, ch 1, (3 dc, ch 1, tr) in beg ch-sp—Six 3-dc groups, 7 ch-1 sps, and 2 tr (three 3-dc groups and 3 ch-1 sps on each side of corner ch-1 sp).

Row 4 Ch 5 (counts as tr, ch 1), turn, [3 dc in next ch-1 sp, ch 1] 3 times, (3 dc, ch 1, 3 dc) in corner ch-1 sp, [ch 1, 3 dc in next ch-1 sp] twice, ch 1, (3 dc, ch 1, tr) in beg ch-sp—eight 3-dc groups, 9 ch-1 sps, and 2 tr (four 3-dc groups and 4 ch-1 sps on each side of corner ch-1 sp). Fasten off.

Row 5 (WS) Draw up a loop of 3rd color of color sequence in first tr, ch 5 (counts as tr, ch 1), [3 dc in next ch-1 sp, ch 1] 4 times, (3 dc, ch 1, 3 dc) in corner ch-1 sp, [ch 1, 3 dc in next ch-1 sp] 3 times, ch 1, (3 dc, ch 1, tr) in beg ch-sp—ten 3-dc groups, 11 ch-1 sps, and 2 tr (five 3-dc groups and 5 ch-1 sps on each side of corner ch-1 sp).

Row 6 Ch 5 (counts as tr, ch 1), turn, [3 dc in next ch-1 sp, ch 1] 5 times, (3 dc, ch 1, 3 dc) in corner ch-1 sp, [ch 1, 3 dc in next ch-1 sp] 4 times, ch 1, (3 dc, ch 1, tr) in beg ch-sp—twelve 3-dc groups, 13 ch-1 sps, and 2 tr (six 3-dc groups and 6 ch-1 sps on each side of corner ch-1 sp). Fasten off.

FINISHING

Block Squares to approx 6½"/16.5cm square.
Block Triangles so side edges measure approx 6½"/16.5cm and diagonal edge measures approx 9"/23cm.
Sew Squares and Triangles together following Layout Diagram.

TRIM

From RS, draw up a loop of A in top corner sp, so that you are ready to work along top edge of Shawl.

Rnd 1 (RS) Ch 4 (counts as dc, ch 1), working in ends of rows along top edge, work 3 dc in end of Row 6 of first Triangle, *[ch 1, sk next row, 3 dc in end of next row] twice, ch 1, sk next row, 3 dc in center ch of Triangle, [ch 1, sk next row, 3 dc in end of next row] 3 times, ch 1, sk seam between Triangle, 3 dc in end of next row;

rep from * across top edge ending after working 3 dc in corner sp at end of Row 6 of last Triangle, ch 1, 3 dc in same corner sp (corner made); working along side edge, **(ch 1, 3 dc in next ch-1 sp) to corner ch-1 sp before seam between pieces, ch 1, dc in corner ch-1 sp of current piece, dc in seam between pieces, dc in corner ch-1 sp of next piece; rep from ** around working (3 dc, ch 1, 3 dc) in lower corner ch-1 sp, work 2 more dc in beg corner sp (first corner completed); join with loose sl st in beg ch-4. Fasten off.

Rnd 2 From RS, draw up a loop of B in any corner ch-sp, ch 4 (counts as dc, ch 1), 3 dc in same corner ch-sp, *ch 1, 3 dc in next ch-1 sp; rep from * around working (3 dc, ch 1, 3 dc) in corner ch-1 sps, work 2 more dc in beg corner ch-sp; join with loose sl st in beg ch-4. Fasten off.

Rnd 3 With C, work same as Rnd 2, do not fasten off at end of rnd.

Rnd 4 (WS) With C, ch 1, turn, sc in each dc and ch-1 sp around working 3 sc in corner ch-1 sps; join with sl st in first sc.

Rnd 5 (WS) With C, do not turn, sl st in each sc around. Fasten off.

Weave in ends. Block lightly. •

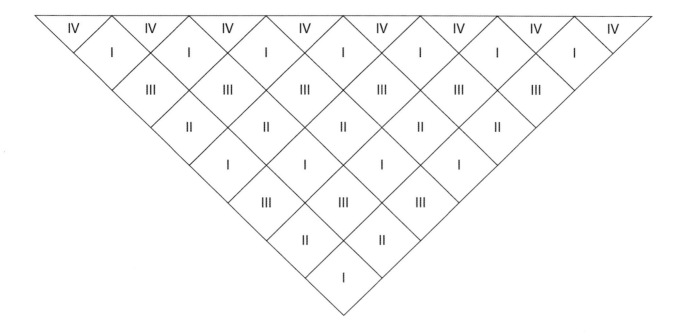

Granny Square Jacket

Easy

SIZES
S (M, L, 1X, 2X).

MEASUREMENTS
Finished Bust Approx 39 (42, 45, 48, 51)"/99 (106.5, 114.5, 122, 129.5)cm
Finished Length (exluding body trim) Approx 22¾ (24½, 26¼, 28, 29¾)"/58 (62, 66.5, 71, 75.5)cm

MATERIALS
YARN
LION BRAND® 24/7 Cotton®, 3½oz/100g balls, each approx 186yd/170m (cotton)
- 5 (6, 7, 8, 9) balls in #116 Succulent (A)
- 2 (2, 3, 3, 4) balls each in #156 Mint (B) and #158 Goldenrod (C)

HOOK
- Size H-8 (5mm) crochet hook, *or size to obtain gauge*

NOTIONS
- Tapestry needle

GAUGE
Rnds 1–5 of Square = approx 6"/15cm square.
BE SURE TO CHECK YOUR GAUGE.

NOTES
1) Jacket is made from 29 Squares and 6 Half Squares.
2) Squares are worked in joined rounds with Right Side always facing. Do not turn at beginning of rounds.
3) Half Squares are worked back and forth in rows.
4) Finished Squares and Half Squares are sewn together following a diagram to make the Jacket.

JACKET
SQUARES (MAKE 29)
With B, ch 4; join with sl st in first ch to form a ring.
Rnd 1 (RS) Ch 4 (counts as dc, ch 1), [3 dc in ring, ch 1] 3 times, 2 dc in ring; join with loose sl st in beg ch-4 sp—you will have 12 dc and 4 ch-1 sps in this rnd.
Rnd 2 Ch 4 (counts as dc, ch 1), 3 dc in beg ch-4 sp (same ch-sp as joining sl st), *ch 1, (3 dc, ch 1, 3 dc) in next ch-1 sp (corner made); rep from * 2 more times, ch 1, work 2 more dc in beg ch-4 sp; join with loose sl st in beg ch-4 sp—24 dc and 8 ch-1 sps (two 3-dc groups and 1 ch-1 sp along each of 4 sides between corner ch-1 sps). Fasten off.
Rnd 3 From RS, join C with sl st in any corner ch-1 sp, ch 4 (counts as dc, ch 1), 3 dc in same corner ch-1 sp, *ch 1, 3 dc in next ch-1 sp, ch 1, (3 dc, ch 1, 3 dc) in next corner ch-1 sp; rep from * 2 more times, ch 1, 3 dc in next ch-1 sp, ch 1, work 2 more dc in beg ch-4 sp; join with loose sl st in beg ch-4 sp—three 3-dc groups and 2 ch-1 sps along each of 4 sides between corner ch-1 sps. Fasten off.
Rnd 4 From RS, join A with sl st in any corner ch-1 sp, ch 4 (counts as dc, ch 1), 3 dc in same corner ch-1 sp, *[ch 1, 3 dc in next ch-1 sp] twice, ch 1, (3 dc, ch 1, 3 dc) in next corner ch-1 sp; rep from * 2 more times, [ch 1, 3 dc in next ch-1 sp] twice, ch 1, work 2 more dc in beg ch-4 sp; join with loose sl st in beg ch-4 sp—four 3-dc groups and 3 ch-1 sps along each of 4 sides between corner ch-1 sps.
Next 1 (2, 2, 3, 3) Rnd(s) Ch 4 (counts as dc, ch 1), 3 dc in beg ch-4 sp, *(ch 1, 3 dc in next ch-1 sp) to next corner ch-1 sp, ch 1, (3 dc, ch 1, 3 dc) in next corner ch-1 sp; rep from * 2 more times, (ch 1, 3 dc in next ch-1 sp) to next corner ch-1 sp, ch 1, work 2 more dc in beg ch-4 sp; join with loose sl st in beg ch-4 sp—5 (6, 6, 7, 7) 3-dc groups and 4 (5, 5, 6, 6) ch-1 sps along each of 4 sides between corner ch-1 sps in last rnd.

Granny Square Jacket

Sizes S (L, 2X) only
Next Rnd Ch 1, sc in beg ch-4 sp, sc in each dc and ch-1 sp around; join with sl st in first sc—19 (23, 27) sc along each of 4 sides between corner sc. Fasten off.

Sizes M (1X) only
Fasten off.

HALF SQUARES (MAKE 6)
Row 1 (WS) With B, ch 4, (dc, ch 1, 3 dc, ch 1, 2 dc) in 4th ch from hook (3 skipped ch count as dc)—you will have 7 dc and 2 ch-1 sps in this row.

Row 2 (RS) Ch 4 (counts as dc, ch 1), turn, (3 dc, ch 1, 3 dc) in next ch-1 sp (corner made), ch 1, (3 dc, ch 1, 3 dc) in next ch-1 sp (corner made), ch 1, dc in 3rd ch of beg ch-4—14 dc and 5 ch-1 sps. Fasten off.

Row 3 From WS, join C with sl st in first dc, ch 3 (counts as dc), dc in next ch-1 sp, ch 1, (3 dc, ch 1, 3 dc) in next corner ch-1 sp, ch 1, 3 dc in next ch-1 sp, ch 1, (3 dc, ch 1, 3 dc) in next corner ch-1 sp, ch 1, dc in beg ch-4 sp, dc in 3rd ch of beg ch-4—19 dc and 6 ch-1 sps. Fasten off.

Row 4 From RS, join A with sl st in first dc, ch 4 (counts as dc, ch 1), 3 dc in next ch-1 sp, ch 1, (3 dc, ch 1, 3 dc) in next corner ch-1 sp, [ch 1, 3 dc in next ch-1 sp] twice, ch 1, (3 dc, ch 1, 3 dc) in next corner ch-1 sp, ch 1, 3 dc in next ch-1 sp, ch 1, dc in top of beg ch-3—26 dc and 9 ch-1 sps.

Row 5 Ch 3 (counts as dc), turn, dc in next ch-1 sp, ch 1, 3 dc in next ch-1 sp, ch 1, (3 dc, ch 1, 3 dc) in next corner ch-1 sp, (ch 1, 3 dc in next ch-1 sp) to next corner ch-1 sp, ch 1, (3 dc, ch 1, 3 dc) in next corner ch-1 sp, ch 1, 3 dc in next ch-1 sp, ch 1, dc in beg ch-4 sp, dc in 3rd ch of beg ch-4—31 dc and 10 ch-1 sps.

Size S only
Row 6 (RS) Ch 1, turn, sc in each dc and ch-1 sp across—41 sc (19 sc between corner sc). Fasten off.

Size M only
Row 6 (RS) From RS, join A with sl st in first dc, ch 4 (counts as dc, ch 1), [3 dc in next ch-1 sp, ch 1] twice, (3 dc, ch 1, 3 dc) in next corner ch-1 sp, [ch 1, 3 dc in next ch-1 sp] 4 times, ch 1, (3 dc, ch 1, 3 dc) in next corner ch-1 sp, [ch 1, 3 dc in next ch-1 sp] twice, ch 1, dc in top of beg ch-3—38 dc and 13 ch-1 sps (six 3-dc groups and 5 ch-1 sps between corner ch-1 sps). Fasten off.

Size L only
Row 6 (RS) Work same as Row 6 for size M.
Row 7 Ch 1, turn, sc in each dc and ch-1 sp across—51 sc (23 sc between corner sc). Fasten off.

Size 1X only
Row 6 Work same as Row 6 for size M.
Row 7 Ch 3 (counts as dc), turn, dc in next ch-1 sp, [ch 1, 3 dc in next ch-1 sp] twice, ch 1, (3 dc, ch 1, 3 dc) in next corner ch-1 sp, (ch 1, 3 dc in next ch-1 sp) to next corner ch-1 sp, ch 1, (3 dc, ch 1, 3 dc) in next corner ch-1 sp, [ch 1, 3 dc in next ch-1 sp] twice, ch 1, dc in beg ch-4 sp, dc in 3rd ch of beg ch-4—43 dc and 14 ch-1 sps (seven 3-dc groups and 6 ch-1 sps between corner ch-1 sps). Fasten off.

Size 2X only
Rows 6 and 7 Work same as Rows 6 and 7 for size 1X.
Row 8 Ch 1, turn, sc in each dc and ch-1 sp across—57 sc (27 sc between corner sc). Fasten off.

FINISHING
Block Squares to 6 (7, 7½, 8)"/16.5 (18, 19, 20.5, 21.5)cm. Block Half Squares to the same length and half the width of the Squares.
Sew Squares and Half Squares together following diagram.
Sew side and sleeve seams.

SLEEVE TRIM
Note Rnd 1 of sleeve trim is worked in sts of last rnd of Squares at wrist edge. If making size S, L or 2X, in Rnd 1 when instructed to work into a ch-1 sp, work into the sc in the last rnd immediately above the ch-1 sp.

Rnd 1 (RS) From RS, join B with sl st in any ch-1 sp of one sleeve edge, ch 3 (counts as dc), 2 dc in same ch-1 sp, *ch 1, 3 dc in next ch-1 sp or seam between Squares; rep from * around, ch 1; join with sl st in top of beg ch-3.

Rnd 2 Turn, sl st in first ch-1 sp, ch 3 (counts as dc), 2 dc in same ch-1 sp, *ch 1, 3 dc in next ch-1 sp; rep from * around, ch 1; join with sl st in top of beg ch-3. Fasten off.

Rnd 3 From RS join C with sl st in any ch-1 sp, ch 3 (counts as dc), 2 dc in same ch-1 sp, , *ch 1, 3 dc in next ch-1 sp; rep from * around, ch 1; join with sl st in top of beg ch-3.
Fasten off.
Rep around 2nd sleeve edge.

BODY TRIM

Note If making size S, L, or 2X, in Rnd 1 when instructed to work into a ch-1 sp, work into the sc in the last rnd immediately above the ch-1 sp.

Rnd 1 (RS) From RS, join B with sl st in any ch-1 sp of lower back edge, ch 3 (counts as dc), 2 dc in same ch-1 sp, *ch 1, 3 dc in next ch-1 sp or seam between Squares; rep from * all the way along lower edge, up front edge, around neck edge, down opposite front edge and along remaining lower edge, working (3 dc, ch 1, 3 dc) in front lower and top corners, ch 1; join with sl st in top of beg ch-3.

Notes When working along front edges, work (ch 1, 3 dc) pattern as evenly spaced as possible. At inner corners of neck opening, work a dc in the corner ch-1 sp of all 3 of the adjoining corners.

Rnds 2 and 3 Work same as Rnds 2 and 3 of sleeve trim. Fasten off.

Weave in ends. •

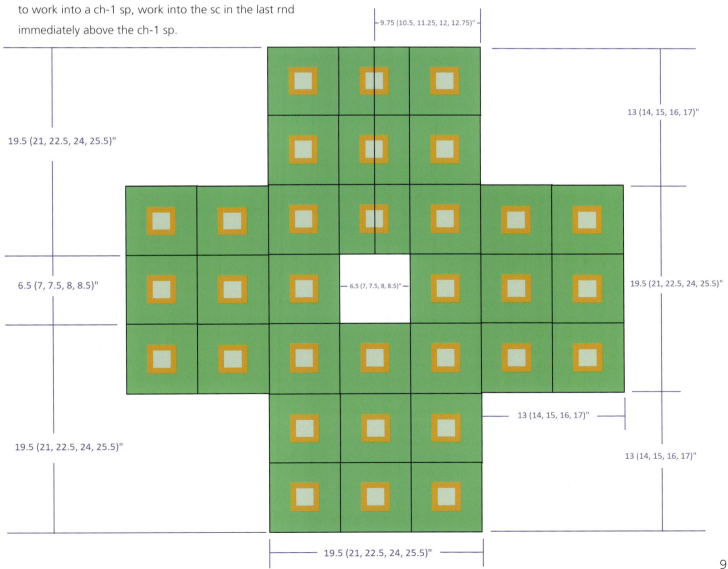

Bobby Granny Square Blanket

Easy

MEASUREMENTS
Approx 48 x 60"/122 x 152.5cm

MATERIALS
YARN
LION BRAND® Heartland®, 5oz/142g balls, each approx 251yd/230m (acrylic/rayon)
- 2 balls each in #134 Gateway Arch (A) and #154 Petrified Forest (D)
- 4 balls in #122 Grand Canyon (B)
- 3 balls in #149 Great Smoky Mountains (C)

HOOK
- Size I-9 (5.5mm) crochet hook, *or size to obtain gauge*

NOTIONS
- Tapestry needle

GAUGE
1 Granny Square = approx 6"/15cm square.
BE SURE TO CHECK YOUR GAUGE.

NOTES
1) 80 Granny Squares are worked separately, then crocheted together following a diagram.
2) Granny Squares are worked in joined rounds, with the Right Side always facing you. Do not turn at beginning of rounds.
3) Yarn color is changed following Color Sequences. To change yarn color, fasten off at end of round and join new color in any corner to begin next round. To help keep Granny Squares square, join in a different corner at beginning of each round.
4) A border is worked all the way around outside edge of Blanket.

COLOR SEQUENCES
COLOR SEQUENCE I
Work 1 rnd with A, 1 rnd with B, 1 rnd with C, and 2 rnds with D.

COLOR SEQUENCE II
Work 1 rnd with D, 1 rnd with A, 1 rnd with B, and 2 rnds with C.

COLOR SEQUENCE III
Work 1 rnd with C, 1 rnd with D, 1 rnd with A, and 2 rnds with B.

COLOR SEQUENCE IV
Work 1 rnd with B, 1 rnd with C, 1 rnd with D, and 2 rnds with A.

BLANKET
GRANNY SQUARES (MAKE 80—20 IN EACH OF THE 4 COLOR SEQUENCES)
With first color, ch 3; join with sl st in first ch to form a ring.

Rnd 1 (RS) Ch 3 (counts as dc), 2 dc in ring, [ch 2, 3 dc in ring] 3 times, ch 2; join with sl st in top of beg ch-3—you will have 12 dc and 4 ch-2 sps in this rnd.
Fasten off.

Rnd 2 From RS, draw up a loop of 2nd color in any ch-2 sp of Rnd 1, ch 3 (counts as dc), (2 dc, ch 2, 3 dc) in same ch-2 sp (first corner made), *ch 1, (3 dc, ch 2, 3 dc) in next ch-2 sp (corner made); rep from * 2 more times, ch 1; join with sl st in top of beg ch-3—24 dc, 4 ch-1 sps, and 4 corner ch-2 sps (6 dc and 1 ch-1 sp along each of 4 sides between ch-2 corner sps).
Fasten off.

Bobby Granny Square Blanket

Rnd 3 From RS, draw up a loop of 3rd color in any corner ch-2 sp of Rnd 2, ch 3, (2 dc, ch 2, 3 dc) in same ch-2 sp, ch 1, 3 dc in next ch-1 sp, *ch 1, (3 dc, ch 2, 3 dc) in next corner ch-2 sp, ch 1, 3 dc in next ch-1 sp; rep from * 2 more times, ch 1; join with sl st in top of beg ch-3—36 dc, 8 ch-1 sps, and 4 corner ch-2 sps (9 dc and 2 ch-1 sps along each of 4 sides between corner ch-2 sps).
Fasten off.

Rnd 4 From RS, draw up a loop of 4th color in any corner ch-2 sp of Rnd 3, ch 3, (2 dc, ch 2, 3 dc) in same ch-2 sp, [ch 1, 3 dc in next ch-1 sp] twice, *ch 1, (3 dc, ch 2, 3 dc) in next corner ch-2 sp, [ch 1, 3 dc in next ch-1 sp] twice; rep from * 2 more times, ch 1; join with sl st in top of beg ch-3—48 dc, 12 ch-1 sps, and 4 corner ch-2 sps (12 dc and 3 ch-1 sps along each of 4 sides between corner ch-2 sps).
Do not fasten off.

Rnd 5 Ch 1, sc in each st and ch-1 sp around, work 3 sc in each corner ch-2 sp; join with sl st in first sc—72 sc.
Fasten off.

FINISHING

Following diagram, arrange Granny Squares into 10 rows of 8 Squares each.

Crochet edges of 8 Squares of one row tog, working each seam as follows: From RS with B, beg at one end of edge and working in back loops only of both thicknesses, sl st across edge. Rep until all 8 Squares are joined together to make a strip.

Rep to make a total 10 strips.

Rep to join side edges of strips together.

BORDER

From RS, join B with sl st in any ch-2 corner sp of Blanket.
Rnd 1 (RS) Working in back loops only, ch 1, sc in each st and ch-sp around outside edge of Blanket, working 3 sc in each corner; join with sl st in first sc.

Rnd 2 Ch 3 (counts as dc), dc in each st around, working 3 dc in center sc of each 3-sc corner; join with sl st in top of beg ch-3.
Fasten off.

Rnd 3 From RS, draw up a loop of C in center dc of any 3-dc corner, ch 1, 3 sc in same st, sc in each st around working 3 sc in center dc of each 3-dc corner; join with sl st in first sc.
Fasten off.

Weave in ends. •

4	3	1	2	4	3	1	2
1	2	3	4	1	2	3	4
3	4	2	1	3	4	2	1
2	1	4	3	2	1	4	3
4	3	1	2	4	3	1	2
1	2	3	4	1	2	3	4
3	4	2	1	3	4	2	1
2	1	4	3	2	1	4	3
4	3	1	2	4	3	1	2
1	2	3	4	1	2	3	4

Gramercy Granny Scarf

Easy

MEASUREMENTS
Approx 8 x 64"/20.5 x 162.5cm

MATERIALS
YARN
LION BRAND® Hometown®, 5oz/142g balls, each approx 81yd/74m (acrylic) 6
- 2 balls in #153 Oakland Black (A)
- 1 ball each in #149 Dallas Grey (B), #114 Tampa Spice (C), #172 Oklahoma City Green (D), #109 Fort Worth Blue (E), #175 Montpelier Peacock (F), #136 Portsmouth Pumpkin (G), and #159 Madison Mustard (H)

HOOK
- Size N (10mm) crochet hook, *or size to obtain gauge*

NOTIONS
- Tapestry needle

GAUGE
One Square = approx 8"/20.5cm square.
BE SURE TO CHECK YOUR GAUGE.

NOTES
1) 8 Squares are worked separately, then sewn together to make the Scarf.
2) Each Square is worked in joined rounds with the Right Side always facing.
3) Rounds 1–3 are worked with yarn colors B, C, D, E, F, G, and H, as desired. Round 4 is worked with A.
4) For those who find a visual helpful, we've included a stitch diagram for the Square.

SCARF
SQUARES (MAKE 8)
Rnd 1 With any color except A, ch 3 (counts as dc), 2 dc in ring, [ch 2, 3 dc in ring] 3 times, ch 2; join with sl st in top of beg ch-3—you will have 12 dc and 4 ch-2 sps. Fasten off.
Rnd 2 Join 2nd yarn color with a sl st in any ch-2 sp, ch 3 (counts as dc), 2 dc in same ch-2 sp, *ch 1, (3 dc, ch 2, 3 dc) in next ch-2 sp (corner made); rep from * 2 more times, ch 1, 3 dc again in first ch-2 sp, ch 2; join with sl st

Gramercy Granny Scarf

in top of beg ch-3—24 dc, 4 ch-1 sps, and 4 corner ch-2 sps (2 (3-dc groups) and 1 ch-1 sp along each of 4 sides between corner ch-2 sps).

Fasten off.

Note To maintain the square shape, join each new yarn color in a different corner ch-2 sp.

Rnd 3 Join 3rd yarn color with a sl st in any corner ch-2 sp, ch 3 (counts as dc), 2 dc in same ch-2 sp, *ch 1, 3 dc in next ch-1 sp, ch 1, (3 dc, ch 2, 3 dc) in next corner ch-2 sp; rep from * 2 more times, ch 1, 3 dc in next ch-1 sp, ch 1, 3 dc again in first corner ch-2 sp, ch 2; join with sl st in top of beg ch-3—36 dc, 8 ch-1 sps, and 4 corner ch-2 sps (3 (3-dc groups) and 2 ch-1 sps along each of 4 sides between corner ch-2 sps).

Fasten off.

Rnd 4 Join A with a sl st in any corner ch-2 sp, ch 3 (counts as dc), 2 dc in same ch-2 sp, *[ch 1, 3 dc in next ch-1 sp] twice, ch 1, (3 dc, ch 2, 3 dc) in next corner ch-2 sp; rep from * 2 more times, [ch 1, 3 dc in next ch-1 sp] twice, ch 1, 3 dc again in first corner ch-2 sp, ch 2; join with sl st in top of beg ch-3—48 dc, 8 ch-1 sps, and 4 corner ch-2 sps (4 (3-dc groups) and 3 ch-1 sps along each of 4 sides between corner ch-2 sps).

Fasten off, leaving a long yarn tail.

FINISHING

Sew Squares together to make the Scarf. Weave in ends.

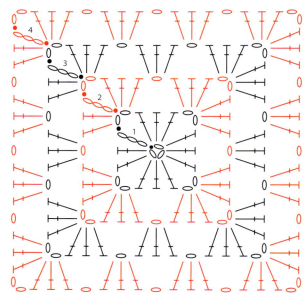

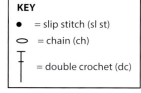

KEY
- ● = slip stitch (sl st)
- ○ = chain (ch)
- ╂ = double crochet (dc)

Urban Granny Dog Sweater

Easy

SIZES
S (M, L, XL).

MEASUREMENTS
Finished Chest 11¼ (19½, 25½, 30½)"/28.5 (49.5, 65, 77.5)cm
Finished Length 10½ (17, 22½, 27½)"/26.5 (43, 57, 70)cm

MATERIALS
YARN
LION BRAND® Wool-Ease® Thick & Quick®, 6oz/170g balls, each approx 106yd/97m (acrylic/wool)
- 1 (1, 1, 2) balls each in #136 Apricot (A) and #178 Cilantro (B)

HOOK
- Size P-15 (10mm) crochet hook, *or size to obtain gauge*

NOTIONS
- Tapestry needle

GAUGE
6 hdc + 5 rows = 4"/10cm.
BE SURE TO CHECK YOUR GAUGE.

SWEATER
BACK
With A, ch 4; join with sl st in first ch to form a ring.
Rnd 1 Ch 2 (counts as hdc), hdc in ring, *ch 2, 2 hdc in ring; rep from * 2 more times, ch 2; join B with sl st in top of beg ch.
Rnd 2 Sl st to first ch-2 sp, ch 2 (counts as hdc here and throughout), hdc in same ch-2 sp, *ch 2, 2 hdc in same ch-2 sp, ch 1, 2 hdc in next ch-2 sp; rep from * 2 more times, ch 2, 2 hdc in same ch-2 sp, ch 1; join A with sl st in top of beg ch.
Rnd 3 Sl st to first ch-2 sp, ch 2, hdc in same ch-2 sp, *ch 2, 2 hdc in same ch-2 sp, [ch 1, 2 hdc in next ch-sp] 2 times; rep from * 2 more times, ch 2, 2 hdc in same ch-2 sp, ch 1, 2 hdc in next ch-sp, ch 1; join B with sl st in top of beg ch.
Rnd 4 Sl st to first ch-2 sp, ch 2, hdc in same ch-2 sp, *ch 2, 2 hdc in same ch-2 sp, ch 1, [2 hdc in next ch-sp, ch 1] across to next ch-2 sp, 2 hdc in ch-2 sp; rep from * 2 more times, ch 2, 2 hdc in same ch-2 sp, [ch 1, 2 hdc in next ch-sp] across to beg ch, ch 1; join A with sl st in top of beg ch.
Rep last Rnd 1 (4, 7, 9) times. Fasten off.

Urban Granny Dog Sweater

UNDERPIECE
Work as for Back for 2 (4, 5, 6) rnds. Do not fasten off.

Neck
With A, Sl st to first ch-2 sp.
Rnd 1 Ch 2, hdc in each hdc and ch-sp on one edge of Underpiece, hdc in each hdc and ch-sp along one edge of Back; join with sl st in top of beg ch.
Rnd 2 Ch 2, hdc in each hdc around; join with sl st in top of beg ch.
Rep last rnd 1 (3, 4, 6) more times.
Fasten off.

Sew sides of Underpiece to Back, leaving 3 (3½, 4, 4½)"/7.5 (9, 10, 11.5)cm open on each side for legs. Weave in ends. •

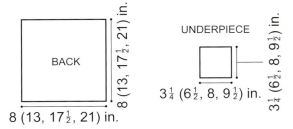

Diagonal Granny Afghan

Easy

MEASUREMENTS
42 x 52"/106.5 x 132cm

MATERIALS

YARN
LION BRAND® Vanna's Choice®, 3½oz/100g balls, each approx 170yd/156m (acrylic)
• 11 balls in #099 Linen

HOOK
• Size J-10 (6mm) crochet hook, *or size to obtain gauge*

NOTIONS
• Tapestry needle
• 4"/10cm piece of heavy cardboard

GAUGE
Basic Square = 5¾"/14.5cm measured diagonally from corner to corner.
BE SURE TO CHECK YOUR GAUGE.

STITCH GLOSSARY

sc2tog (sc decrease) Insert hook into st and draw up a loop. Insert hook into next st and draw up a loop. Yarn over, draw through all 3 loops on hook.

BLANKET

BASIC SQUARE (MAKE 111)
Ch 3; join with sl st in first ch to form ring.
Rnd 1 (RS) Ch 3 (counts as first dc here and throughout), work 2 more dc in ring, [ch 3, 3 dc in ring] 3 times, ch 3; join with sl st in top of beg ch.
Rnd 2 Sl st to first ch-3 sp, ch 3, (2 dc, ch 3, 3 dc) in same ch-3 sp, [ch 1, (3 dc, ch 3, 3 dc) in next ch-3 sp] 3 times, ch 1; join with sl st in top of beg ch.
Rnd 3 Ch 3, dc in next 2 dc, (2 dc, ch 1, 2 dc) in next ch-3 sp, dc in next 3 dc, dc in ch-1 sp, *dc in next 3 dc, (2 dc, ch 1, 2 dc) in next ch-3 sp, dc in next 3 dc, dc in ch-1 sp; rep from * around; join with sl st in top of beg ch. Fasten off.

HALF-SQUARE (MAKE 16)
Ch 3; join with sl st in first ch to form ring.
Row 1 (RS) Ch 4 (counts as dc, ch 1 here and throughout), (3 dc, ch 3, 3 dc) in ring, ch 1, dc in ring.
Row 2 Ch 4, turn, 3 dc in ch-1 sp, ch 1, sk 3 dc, (3 dc, ch 3, 3 dc) in ch-3 sp, ch 1, sk 3 dc, 3 dc in beg ch-4 sp, ch 1, dc in 3rd ch of beg ch.
Row 3 Ch 3, turn, 2 dc in ch-1 sp, dc in next 3 dc, dc in ch-1 sp, dc in next 3 dc, (2 dc, ch 1, 2 dc) in ch-3 sp, dc in next 3 dc, dc in ch-1 sp, dc in next 3 dc, 2 dc in beg ch-4 sp, dc in 3rd ch of beg ch. Fasten off.

17

Diagonal Granny Afghan

FINISHING
Following diagram, sew Basic Squares and Half Squares together.

EDGING
From RS, join yarn with sl st at one corner, ready to work along shaped end of Afghan.
Row 1 *Sc evenly along shaped end, working 3 sc at tip of each point and sc2tog between points; at corner, work sc evenly spaced across long side; rep from * once.

SIDE EDGING
Next Row Working across long side of Afghan only, sc in each sc.
Note Next 3 rows are worked across same long side of Afghan.
Next Row Ch 1, turn, working across long side of Afghan only, sc in each sc.
Rep last row once.
Picot Row Ch 2, turn, sl st in 2nd ch from hook, sk first 2 sc, sl st in next 2 sc, (ch 2, sl st in 2nd ch from hook, sk 1 sc, sl st in next 2 sc) across row.
Fasten off.
From RS, join yarn with sl st at corner, ready to work across remaining long side of Afghan and rep 4 rows of Side Edging.

TASSELS (MAKE 14)
Wrap yarn around cardboard 25 times. Cut a piece of yarn approx 10"/25.5cm long and thread doubled onto tapestry needle. Insert needle under all strands at upper edge of cardboard. Pull tightly and knot securely near strands. Cut yarn loops at lower edge of cardboard. Cut a piece of yarn approx 8"/20.5cm long and wrap tightly around loops 1"/2.5cm below top knot to form Tassel neck. Knot securely; thread ends onto needle and weave ends to center of Tassel. Trim Tassel ends evenly. Sew one Tassel to each outer point at top and bottom edges.

Weave in ends. •

Bellona Granny Shawl

Easy

MEASURMENTS
Approx 28"/71cm square

MATERIALS
YARN
LION BRAND® Summer Nights Bonus Bundle, 7oz/200g balls, each approx 875yd/800m (acrylic/polyester)
- 1 ball in #312 Sunset

HOOK
- Size E-4 (3.5mm) crochet hook, *or size to obtain gauge*

NOTIONS
- Tapestry needle

GAUGE
Rnds 1–7 = approx 4"/10cm square.
BE SURE TO CHECK YOUR GAUGE.

NOTE
Shawl is worked in one piece in joined and turned rounds.

SHAWL
Ch 4, join with a sl st in first ch to make a ring.

Rnd 1 Ch 3 (counts as first dc in this rnd and in all following rnds), 2 dc in ring, [ch 1, 3 dc in ring] 3 times, ch 1; join with sl st in top of beg ch—you will have 4 ch-1 sps and 12 dc (consisting of four 3-dc groups) in this rnd.

Rnd 2 Turn, (sl st, ch 3, 2 dc, ch 1, 3 dc) in first ch-1 sp (first corner made), *(3 dc, ch 1, 3 dc) in next ch-1 sp (corner made); rep from * 2 more times; join with sl st in top of beg ch—4 corner ch-1 sps and 24 dc (eight 3-dc groups).

Rnd 3 Turn, (sl st, ch 3, 2 dc) in first sp between 3-dc groups, *(3 dc, ch 1, 3 dc) in next corner ch-1 sp, 3 dc in next sp between 3-dc groups; rep from * 2 more times, (3 dc, ch 1, 3 dc) in last corner ch-1 sp; join with sl st in top of beg ch—4 corner ch-1 sps and 36 dc (twelve 3-dc groups).

Rnd 4 Turn, (sl st, ch 3, 2 dc) in first sp between 3-dc groups, *(3 dc, ch 1, 3 dc) in next corner ch-1 sp, [3 dc in next sp between 3-dc groups] twice; rep from * 2 more times, (3 dc, ch 1, 3 dc) in next corner ch-1 sp, 3 dc in last sp between 3-dc groups; join with sl st in top of beg ch—4 corner ch-1 sps and 48 dc (sixteen 3-dc groups).

Rnd 5 Turn, (sl st, ch 3, 2 dc) in first sp between 3-dc groups, 3 dc in each sp between 3-dc groups to next corner ch-1 sp, *(3 dc, ch 1, 3 dc) in next corner ch-1 sp, 3 dc in each sp between 3-dc groups to next corner ch-1 sp; rep from * 2 more times, (3 dc, ch 1, 3 dc) in next corner ch-1 sp, 3 dc in each sp between 3-dc groups to end of rnd; join with sl st in top of beg ch—4 corner ch-1 sps and 60 dc (twenty 3-dc groups).

Rep Rnd 5 until you don't have sufficient yarn to do another round.
Fasten off.

FINISHING
Weave in ends. Block to measurements.

Corner Granny Blanket

Easy

MEASUREMENTS
Approx 48"/122cm square

MATERIALS
YARN
LION BRAND® Hometown®, 5oz/142g balls, each approx 81yd/74m (acrylic)
- 1 ball each in #099 Los Angeles Tan (A) and #136 Portsmouth Pumpkin (B)
- 2 balls in #159 Madison Mustard (C)
- 3 balls in #176 Galveston Green (D)
- 3 balls in #175 Montpelier Peacock (E)
- 5 balls in #148 Portland Wine (F)

HOOK
- Size N-13 (9mm) crochet hook, *or size to obtain gauge*

NOTIONS
- Tapestry needle

GAUGE
Three 3-dc groups = approx 5½"/14cm.
BE SURE TO CHECK YOUR GAUGE.

NOTES
1) A Granny Square is made first for corner of Afghan. Work then proceeds back and forth in rows across only 2 sides of the Square.
2) To change color, work last st of old color to last yarn over. Yarn over with new color and draw through all loops on hook to complete stitch. Proceed with new color. Cut old color.

AFGHAN
GRANNY SQUARE
With A, ch 5; join with sl st in first ch to form a ring.

Rnd 1 (RS) Ch 3 (counts as dc here and throughout), 2 dc in ring, [ch 2, 3 dc in ring] 3 times, ch 2; join with sl st in top of beg ch—you will have four 3-dc groups and 4 ch-2 sps at the end of Rnd 1.

Rnd 2 Sl st in next 2 dc, (sl st, ch 3, 2 dc, ch 2, 3 dc) in next ch-2 sp (corner made), *ch 1, (3 dc, ch 2, 3 dc) in next ch-2 sp (corner made); rep from * 2 more times, ch 1; join with sl st in top of beg ch—eight 3-dc groups, 4 corner ch-2 sps, and 4 ch-1 sps.

Rnd 3 Sl st in next 2 dc, (sl st, ch 3, 2 dc, ch 2, 3 dc) in next ch-2 sp, ch 1, 3 dc in next ch-1 sp, *ch 1, (3 dc, ch 2, 3 dc) in next ch-2 sp, ch 1, 3 dc in next ch-1 sp; rep from * 2 more times, ch 1; join with sl st in top of beg ch—twelve 3-dc groups, 4 corner ch-2 sps, and 8 ch-1 sps.

Rnd 4 Sl st in next 2 dc, (sl st, ch 3, 2 dc, ch 2, 3 dc) in next ch-2 sp, [ch 1, 3 dc in next ch-1 sp] twice, *ch 1, (3 dc, ch 2, 3 dc) in next ch-2 sp, [ch 1, 3 dc in next ch-1 sp] twice; rep from * 2 more times, ch 1; join with sl st in top of beg ch—sixteen 3-dc groups, 4 corner ch-2 sps, and 12 ch-1 sps.
Fasten off A.

BAND I
Row 1 (RS) From RS, join B with sl st in any corner ch-2 sp, ch 3, dc in same corner ch-2 sp, [ch 1, 3 dc in next ch-1 sp] to next corner ch-2 sp, ch 1, (3 dc, ch 2, 3 dc) in corner ch-2 sp, [ch 1, 3 dc in next ch-1 sp] to next corner ch-2 sp, ch 1, 2 dc in corner ch-2 sp; leave other 2 sides of Center Square unworked—eight 3-dc groups, two 2-dc groups, 1 corner ch-2 sp, and 8 ch-1 sps.

Corner Granny Blanket

Row 2 Ch 3, turn, 3 dc in next ch-1 sp, [ch 1, 3 dc in next ch-1 sp] to corner ch-2 sp, ch 1, (3 dc, ch 2, 3 dc) in corner ch-2 sp, [ch 1, 3 dc in next ch-1 sp] to end of side, dc in top of beg ch—ten 3-dc groups, 2 dc, 1 corner ch-2 sp, and 8 ch-1 sps.

Row 3 Ch 3, turn, dc in first dc, [ch 1, 3 dc in next ch-1 sp] to corner ch-2 sp, ch 1, (3 dc, ch 2, 3 dc) in ch-2 sp, [ch 1, 3 dc in next ch-1 sp] to end of side, ch 1, 2 dc in top of beg ch—ten 3-dc groups, two 2-dc groups, 1 corner ch-2 sp, and 10 ch-1 sps.

Rows 4 and 5 Rep Rows 2 and 3—at the end of Row 5 you will have twelve 3-dc groups.

Row 6 Rep Row 2 and change to C in last st—fourteen 3-dc groups.

BAND II

Row 7 With C, rep Row 3—fourteen 3-dc groups.
Rows 8–13 With C, rep Rows 2 and 3 three times—twenty 3-dc groups in Row 12.
Row 14 With C, rep Row 2 and change to D in last st—twenty-two 3-dc groups.

BAND III

Row 15 With D, rep Row 3—twenty-two 3-dc groups.
Rows 16–23 With D, rep Rows 2 and 3 four times and change to E in last st of Row 23—thirty 3-dc groups in Row 22.

BAND IV

Rows 24–33 With E, rep Rows 2 and 3 five times and change to F in last st of row 33—forty 3-dc groups in Row 32.

BAND V

Rows 34–43 With F, rep Rows 2 and 3 five times—fifty 3-dc groups in Row 42.
Row 44 With F, rep Row 2—fifty-two 3-dc groups. Fasten off.

FINISHING

Weave in ends.

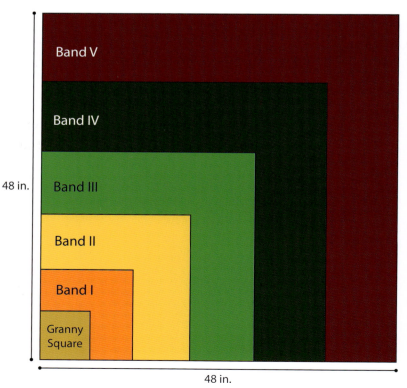

- #099 Los Angeles Tan (A)
- #136 Portsmouth Pumpkin (B)
- #159 Madison Mustard (C)
- #176 Galveston Green (D)
- #175 Montpelier Peacock (E)
- #148 Portland Wine (F)

Granny Motif Market Bag

Easy

MEASUREMENTS
Approx 11 x 13"/28 x 33cm, excluding handles

MATERIALS
YARN
LION BRAND® Vanna's Choice®, 3½oz/100g balls, each approx 170yd/156m (acrylic)
- 1 ball each in #113 Scarlet (A), #099 Linen (B), #107 Sapphire (C), #134 Terracotta (D), and #158 Mustard (E)

HOOK
- Size H-8 (5mm) crochet hook, *or size to obtain gauge*

NOTIONS
- Tapestry needle

GAUGE
One Hexagon = approx 5½"/14cm across.
BE SURE TO CHECK YOUR GAUGE.

STITCH GLOSSARY
3-dc Cl (3 double crochet cluster) Yarn over, insert hook in indicated st, yarn over and draw up a loop, yarn over and draw through 2 loops on hook (2 loops rem on hook), [yarn over, insert hook in same st, yarn over and draw up a loop, yarn over and draw through 2 loops on hook] 2 times (4 loops rem on hook), yarn over and draw through all loops on hook.

4-dc Cl (4 double crochet cluster) Yarn over, insert hook in indicated st, yarn over and draw up a loop, yarn over and draw through 2 loops on hook (2 loops rem on hook), [yarn over, insert hook in same st, yarn over and draw up a loop, yarn over and draw through 2 loops on hook] 3 times (5 loops rem on hook), yarn over, draw through all loops on hook.

Granny Motif Market Bag

NOTES

1) Bag is made from 10 Hexagons, 2 each of 5 different color combinations.
2) Hexagons are worked in the round with Right Side facing at all times. Do not turn at the ends of rounds.
3) Handles are worked in rounds of single crochet, after the Hexagons have been sewn together.

BAG

HEXAGON I (MAKE 2)

With B, ch 6; join with sl st in first ch to form a ring.
Rnd 1 (RS) Ch 2, 3-dc Cl in ring, [ch 3, 4-dc Cl in ring] 5 times, ch 3; join with sl st in top of first cluster—6 clusters at the end of this rnd. Fasten off B.
Rnd 2 With RS facing, join C with sl st in any ch-3 sp, ch 2, (3-dc Cl, ch 3, 4-dc Cl) in same ch-3 sp (corner made), *ch 3, (4-dc Cl, ch 3, 4-dc Cl) in next ch-3 sp (corner made); rep from * 4 more times, ch 3; join with sl st in top of first cluster—12 clusters at the end of this rnd. Fasten off C.
Rnd 3 With RS facing, join D with sl st in any corner ch-3 sp, ch 2, (3-dc Cl, ch 3, 4-dc Cl) in same ch-3 sp (corner made), ch 3, 4-dc Cl in next ch-3 sp, *ch 3, (4-dc Cl, ch 3, 4-dc Cl) in next ch-3 sp (corner made), ch 3, 4-dc Cl in next ch-3 sp; rep from * 4 more times, ch 3; join with sl st in top of first cluster—18 clusters at the end of this rnd. Fasten off D.
Note In next rnd, take care to work dc as instructed, not clusters.
Rnd 4 With RS facing, join E with sl st in any corner ch-3 sp, ch 3 (counts as first dc), (2 dc, ch 2, 3 dc) in same ch-3 sp, 3 dc in each of next 2 ch-3 sps, *(3 dc, ch 2, 3 dc) in next corner ch-3 sp, 3 dc in each of next 2 ch-3 sps; rep from * 4 more times; join with sl st in top of beg ch—72 dc at the end of this rnd.
Fasten off.

HEXAGON II (MAKE 2)

Make same as Hexagon I, using E for Rnd 1, A for Rnd 2, B for Rnd 3, and C for Rnd 4.

HEXAGON III (MAKE 2)

Make same as Hexagon I, using D for Rnd 1, E for Rnd 2, A for Rnd 3, and B for Rnd 4.

HEXAGON IV (MAKE 2)

Make same as Hexagon I, using C for Rnd 1, D for Rnd 2, E for Rnd 3, and A for Rnd 4.

HEXAGON V (MAKE 2)

Make same as Hexagon I, using A for Rnd 1, B for Rnd 2, C for Rnd 3, and D for Rnd 4.

FINISHING

Following Assembly Diagram, whip stitch Hexagons tog. Fold piece along dashed lines, matching A with B, and C with D. Whipstitch side seams.

HANDLES

From RS, join C with a sl st in side seam between Hexagons I and III.
Rnd 1 Ch 1, *work 14 sc evenly spaced across side of Hexagon III to ch-2 sp at top point, ch 72, beg at ch-2 sp at point of Hexagon I, work 14 sc evenly spaced across side of Hexagon I to side seam (first handle made); rep from * for 2nd handle; join with sl st in first sc—144 ch and 56 sc.
Rnd 2 Ch 1, sc in each sc and ch around; join with sl st in first sc.
Rnds 3 and 4 Ch 1, sc in each sc around; join with sl st in first sc.
Fasten off.

EDGING

From RS, join C with sl st in any st on inside edge of first handle. Work sc evenly spaced around inside edge of handle and top edge of Bag; join with sl st in first sc. Fasten off.

Rep edging on 2nd handle.

Weave in ends. •

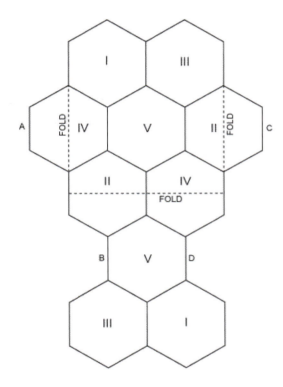

Granny Afghan/Shawl

Easy

MEASUREMENTS
Approx 45"/114.5cm square

MATERIALS
YARN
LION BRAND® Shawl in a Ball®, 5.3oz/150g balls, each approx 481yd/440m (cotton/acrylic/other) (4)
- 1 ball in #201 Restful Rainbow (A)
- 2 balls in #204 Healing Teal (B)

HOOK
- Size I-9 (5.5mm) crochet hook, *or size to obtain gauge*

NOTIONS
- Tapestry needle

GAUGE
Rnds 1–4 = approx 4½"/11.5cm square.
BE SURE TO CHECK YOUR GAUGE.

NOTE
Afghan/Shawl is worked in one piece in joined and turned rounds.

AFGHAN/SHAWL
With A, ch 4; join with sl st in first ch to form a ring.

Rnd 1 (RS) Ch 3 (counts as first dc in this rnd and in all following rnds), 2 dc in ring, [ch 1, 3 dc in ring] 3 times, ch 1; join with sl st in top of beg ch—you will have 4 ch-1 sps and four 3-dc groups in this rnd.

Rnd 2 Turn, (sl st, ch 3, 2 dc, ch 1, 3 dc) in first ch-1 sp (first corner made), *(3 dc, ch 1, 3 dc) in next ch-1 sp (corner made); rep from * 2 more times; join with sl st in top of beg ch—4 corner ch-1 sps and eight 3-dc groups (two 3-dc groups along each of 4 sides between corner ch-1 sps).

Rnd 3 Turn, (sl st, ch 3, 2 dc) in first sp between 3-dc groups, *(3 dc, ch 1, 3 dc) in next corner ch-1 sp, 3 dc in next sp between 3-dc groups; rep from * 2 more times, (3 dc, ch 1, 3 dc) in last corner ch-1 sp; join with sl st in top of beg ch—4 corner ch-1 sps and twelve 3-dc groups (three 3-dc groups along each of 4 sides between corner ch-1 sps).

Rnd 4 Turn, (sl st, ch 3, 2 dc) in first sp between 3-dc groups, *(3 dc, ch 1, 3 dc) in next corner ch-1 sp, [3 dc in next sp between 3-dc groups] twice; rep from * 2 more times, (3 dc, ch 1, 3 dc) in next corner ch-1 sp, 3 dc in last sp between 3-dc groups; join with sl st in top of beg ch—4 corner ch-1 sps and sixteen 3-dc groups (four 3-dc groups along each of 4 sides between corner ch-1 sps).

Rnds 5–23 Turn, (sl st, ch 3, 2 dc) in first sp between 3-dc groups, 3 dc in each sp between 3-dc groups to next corner ch-1 sp, *(3 dc, ch 1, 3 dc) in next corner ch-1 sp, 3 dc in each sp between 3-dc groups to next corner ch-1 sp; rep from * 2 more times, (3 dc, ch 1, 3 dc) in next corner ch-1 sp, 3 dc in each sp between 3-dc groups to end of rnd; join with sl st in top of beg ch—4 corner ch-1 sps and ninety-two 3-dc groups (twenty-three 3-dc groups along each of 4 sides between corner ch-1 sps) at end of Rnd 23. Fasten off.

Rnd 24 (WS) Join B with a sl st in first sp between 3-dc groups following any corner ch-1 sp, ch 3, 2 dc in same sp, 3 dc in each sp between 3-dc groups to next corner ch-1 sp, *(3 dc, ch 1, 3 dc) in next corner ch-1 sp, 3 dc in each sp between 3-dc groups to next corner ch-1 sp; rep from * 2 more times, (3 dc, ch 1, 3 dc) in next corner ch-1 sp, 3 dc in each sp between 3-dc groups to end of rnd; join with sl st in top of beg ch—4 corner ch-1 sps and ninety-six 3-dc groups (twenty-four 3-dc groups along each of 4 sides between corner ch-1 sps).

Granny Afghan Shawl

Rnds 25–40 With B, rep Rnd 5 sixteen times—4 corner ch-1 sps and one hundred-sixty 3-dc groups (forty 3-dc groups along each of 4 sides between corner ch-1 sps) at the end of Rnd 40.

Rnd 41 Turn, (sl st, ch 3, sl st) in first sp between 3-dc groups, *ch 3, (sl st, ch 3, sl st) in next sp between 3-dc groups or next corner ch-1 sp; rep from * around, ch 3; join with sl st in first sl st. Fasten off.

FINISHING

Weave in ends. •

Granny Square Dish Cloth

Easy

MEASUREMENTS
Approx 10"/25.5cm square

MATERIALS
YARN
LION BRAND® 24/7 Cotton®, 3½oz/100g balls, each approx 186yd/170m (cotton)
- 1 ball each in #098 Ecru (A), #178 Jade (B), #109 Navy (C), #186 Amber (D), and #142 Rose (E)

HOOK
- Size H-8 (5mm) crochet hook, *or size to obtain gauge*

NOTIONS
- Tapestry needle

GAUGE
1 Granny Square = approx 4½"/11.5cm square.
BE SURE TO CHECK YOUR GAUGE.

STITCH GLOSSARY
rev-sc (reverse single crochet) Single crochet worked from left to right (right to left, if left-handed). Insert hook into next stitch to the right (left), under loop on hook, and draw up a loop. Yarn over and draw through all loops on hook.

NOTES
1) Dish Cloth is made from 4 Granny Squares sewn together.
2) Each Granny Square is worked in joined rounds with Right Side always facing. Do not turn at the beginning of rounds.
3) Each round of Granny Square is worked using a different yarn color, following Color Sequences. Change yarn color by fastening off old color and joining new color, as instructed.
4) Edging is worked all the way around outer edge of Dish Cloth.

COLOR SEQUENCES
COLOR SEQUENCE I
Work 1 rnd with B, 1 rnd with C, 1 rnd with D, and 1 rnd with A.

Granny Square Dish Cloth

COLOR SEQUENCE II
Work 1 rnd with C, 1 rnd with E, 1 rnd with B, and 1 rnd with A.

COLOR SEQUENCE III
Work 1 rnd with D, 1 rnd with E, 1 rnd with B, and 1 rnd with A.

COLOR SEQUENCE IV
Work 1 rnd with E, 1 rnd with B, 1 rnd with C, and 1 rnd with A.

DISH CLOTH

GRANNY SQUARES (MAKE 4—1 IN EACH COLOR SEQUENCE)
With first color, ch 3.

Rnd 1 (RS) With first color, 2 dc in 3rd ch from hook (2 skipped ch count as dc), [ch 2, 3 dc in same ch] 3 times, ch 2; join with sl st in top of beg ch-2—you will have 12 dc and 4 ch-2 sps in this rnd.
Fasten off.

Rnd 2 From RS, draw up a loop of second color in any ch-2 sp, ch 2 (counts as dc), 2 dc in same ch-2 sp, *ch 2, (3 dc, ch 2, 3 dc) in next ch-2 sp (corner made); rep from * 2 more times, ch 2, 3 dc in first ch-2 sp, ch 2; join with sl st in top of beg ch-2 (first corner completed)—24 dc and 8 ch-2 sps (two 3-dc groups and 1 ch-2 sp along each of 4 sides between corner ch-2 sps).
Fasten off.

Rnd 3 From RS, draw up a loop of third color in any corner ch-2 sp, ch 2 (counts as dc), 2 dc in same corner ch-2 sp, *ch 2, 3 dc in next ch-2 sp, ch 2, (3 dc, ch 2, 3 dc) in next corner ch-2 sp; rep from * 2 more times, ch 2, 3 dc in next ch-2 sp, ch 2, 3 dc in first corner ch-2 sp, ch 2; join with sl st in top of beg ch-2—36 dc and 12 ch-2 sps (three 3-dc groups and 2 ch-2 sps along each of 4 sides between corner ch-2 sps).
Fasten off.

Rnd 4 From RS, draw up a loop of fourth color in any corner ch-2 sp, ch 2 (counts as dc), 2 dc in same corner ch-2 sp, *[ch 2, 3 dc in next ch-2 sp] twice, ch 2, (3 dc, ch 2, 3 dc) in next corner ch-2 sp; rep from * 2 more times, [ch 2, 3 dc in next ch-2 sp] twice, ch 2, 3 dc in first corner ch-2 sp, ch 2; join with sl st in top of beg ch-2—48 dc and 16 ch-2 sps (four 3-dc groups and 3 ch-2 sps along each of 4 sides between corner ch-2 sps).
Fasten off.

FINISHING
Weave in ends. Block Granny Squares.
From RS with A, sew Granny Squares tog into a square that is 2 Granny Squares wide and 2 Granny Squares high, placing colors as desired.

EDGING
Rnd 1 (RS) From RS, draw up a loop of A in any corner ch-2 sp, ch 2 (counts as dc), work dc as evenly spaced as possible along sides of Square, working 5 dc in each corner ch-2 sp; join with sl st in top of beg ch-2.

Note An optional hanging loop is included in Rnd 2 instruction. If no hanging loop is desired, simply join last rev-sc to beg ch-1, skipping over the instruction for hanging loop.

Rnd 2 Ch 1, rev-sc in each st around; for optional hanging loop, work a chain approx 3"/7.5cm long; join with sl st in beg ch-1.
Fasten off. •

Granny Square Dish Towel

Easy

MEASUREMENTS
Approx 18 x 24"/45.5 x 61cm

MATERIALS
YARN
LION BRAND® 24/7 Cotton®, 3½oz/100g balls, each approx 186yd/170m (cotton)
- 3 balls in #098 Ecru (A)
- 2 ball each in #178 Jade (B), #109 Navy (C), #186 Amber (D), and #142 Rose (E)

HOOK
- Size H-8 (5mm) crochet hook, *or size to obtain gauge*

NOTIONS
- Tapestry needle

GAUGE
1 Granny Square = approx 4½"/11.5cm.
BE SURE TO CHECK YOUR GAUGE.

STITCH GLOSSARY
rev-sc (reverse single crochet) Single crochet worked from left to right (right to left, if left-handed). Insert hook into next stitch to the right (left), under loop on hook, and draw up a loop. Yarn over and draw through all loops on hook.

NOTES
1) Dish Towel begins with a strip of 4 Granny Squares sewn together. Sections of double crochet are worked along both long edges of the Granny Square strip to form the Towel.
2) Each Granny Square is worked in joined rounds with Right Side always facing. Do not turn at the beginning of rounds.
3) Each round of Granny Square is worked using a different yarn color, following Color Sequences. Change yarn color by fastening off old color and joining new color, as instructed.

COLOR SEQUENCES
COLOR SEQUENCE I
Work 1 rnd with B, 1 rnd with C, 1 rnd with D, and 1 rnd with A.

COLOR SEQUENCE II
Work 1 rnd C, 1 rnd with E, 1 rnd with B, and 1 rnd with A.

Granny Square Dish Towel

COLOR SEQUENCE III
Work 1 rnd with D, 1 rnd with E, 1 rnd with B, and 1 rnd with A.

COLOR SEQUENCE IV
Work 1 rnd with E, 1 rnd with B, 1 rnd with C, and 1 rnd with A.

DISH TOWEL

GRANNY SQUARES (MAKE 4—1 IN EACH COLOR SEQUENCE)
With first color, ch 3.

Rnd 1 (RS) With first color, 2 dc in 3rd ch from hook (2 skipped ch count as dc), [ch 2, 3 dc in same ch] 3 times, ch 2; join with sl st in top of beg ch-2—you will have 12 dc and 4 ch-2 sps in this rnd.
Fasten off.

Rnd 2 From RS, draw up a loop of 2nd color in any ch-2 sp, ch 2 (counts as dc), 2 dc in same ch-2 sp, *ch 2, (3 dc, ch 2, 3 dc) in next ch-2 sp (corner made); rep from * 2 more times, ch 2, 3 dc in first ch-2 sp, ch 2; join with sl st in top of beg ch-2 (first corner completed)—24 dc and 8 ch-2 sps (two 3-dc groups and 1 ch-2 sp along each of 4 sides between corner ch-2 sps).
Fasten off.

Rnd 3 From RS, draw up a loop of 3rd color in any corner ch-2 sp, ch 2 (counts as dc), 2 dc in same corner ch-2 sp, *ch 2, 3 dc in next ch-2 sp, ch 2, (3 dc, ch 2, 3 dc) in next corner ch-2 sp; rep from * 2 more times, ch 2, 3 dc in next ch-2 sp, ch 2, 3 dc in first corner ch-2 sp, ch 2; join with sl st in top of beg ch-2—36 dc and 12 ch-2 sps (three 3-dc groups and 2 ch-2 sps along each of 4 sides between corner ch-2 sps).
Fasten off.

Rnd 4 From RS, draw up a loop of 4th color in any corner ch-2 sp, ch 2 (counts as dc), 2 dc in same corner ch-2 sp, *[ch 2, 3 dc in next ch-2 sp] twice, ch 2, (3 dc, ch 2, 3 dc) in next corner ch-2 sp; rep from * 2 more times, [ch 2, 3 dc in next ch-2 sp] twice, ch 2, 3 dc in first corner ch-2 sp, ch 2; join with sl st in top of beg ch-2—48 dc and 16 ch-2 sps (four 3-dc groups and 3 ch-2 sps along each of 4 sides between corner ch-2 sps).
Fasten off.

FINISHING
Weave in ends. Block Granny Squares.
From RS with A, sew all 4 Granny Squares tog into a strip, placing colors as desired.

FIRST DOUBLE CROCHET SECTION
Row 1 (RS) From RS, draw up a loop of A at beg of one long edge of strip of Granny Squares, ch 2 (counts as dc), work 67 more dc as evenly spaced as possible along long edge—68 dc.

Rows 2–33 Ch 2 (counts as dc), turn, sk first st, dc in each st across working last dc in top of beg ch-2.

Row 34 (Edging) Ch 1, do NOT turn, rev-sc in each st across.
Fasten off.

SECOND DOUBLE CROCHET SECTION
Row 1 (RS) From RS, draw up a loop of A at beg of 2nd long edge of strip of Granny Squares, ch 2 (counts as dc), work 67 more dc as evenly spaced as possible along long edge—68 dc.

Rows 2–13 Ch 2 (counts as dc), turn, sk first st, dc in each st across working last dc in top of beg ch-2.

Row 14 (Edging) Ch 1, do NOT turn, rev-sc in each st across.
Fasten off.

FINISHING
Weave in ends. •

Iconic Granny Couch Afghan

Easy

MEASUREMENTS
Approx 47½ x 63½"/120.5 x 161.5cm

MATERIALS
YARN

LION BRAND® Pound of Love®, 16oz/454g balls, each approx 1,020yd/932m (acrylic) (4)
• 1 ball each in #153 Black (A)
LION BRAND® DIYarn®, 1.05oz/30g balls, each approx 65/60m (acrylic) (4)
• 2 balls each in #101 Pink (B), #142 Burgundy (C), #132 Pumpkin (D), #184 Peach (E), #157 Yellow (F), #178 Teal (G), #124 Camel (H), #113 Red (I), #130 Green (J), and #133 Orange (K)
• 1 ball each in #195 Hot Pink (L), #172 Grass (M), #107 Sky (N), #110 Navy (O), #147 Purple (P), #146 Lilac (Q), #126 Brown (R), #098 Cream (S), #149 Grey (T), and #150 Charcoal (U)

HOOK
• Size H-8 (5mm) crochet hook, *or size to obtain gauge*

Iconic Granny Couch Afghan

NOTIONS
- Tapestry needle

GAUGE
1 Square = approx 5¼"/13.5cm.
BE SURE TO CHECK YOUR GAUGE.

NOTES
1) 108 Squares are worked separately, then sewn together to make the Afghan.
2) Each Square is worked in joined rounds with RS always facing.
3) Use any yarns colors B–U for Rnds 1–4 of each Square. Rnd 5 of each Square is worked with yarn A.
4) Have fun with the yarn colors and arrange the Squares any way you like!
5) A simple single crochet border is worked around the assembled Afghan.
6) For those who find a visual helpful, we've included a stitch diagram.

BLANKET
SQUARES (MAKE 108)
Note Use any 4 yarn colors from colors B–U for each of the first 4 rnds.

With first yarn color, ch 4; join with a sl st in first ch to make a ring.

Rnd 1 (RS) Ch 3 (counts as first dc), 2 dc in ring, [ch 2, 3 dc in ring] 3 times, ch 2; join with sl st in top of beg ch-3—you will have 4 ch-2 sps and 12 dc in this rnd (four 3-dc groups).

Fasten off.

Rnd 2 From RS, join 2nd color with a sl st in any ch-2 sp, ch 3 (counts as dc), 2 dc in same ch-2 sp, (3 dc, ch 2, 3 dc) in next ch-2 sp (corner made), (3 dc, ch 2, 3 dc) in each of next 2 ch-2 sps, 3 dc again in first ch-2 sp, ch 2; join with sl st in top of beg ch-3—24 dc and 4 corner ch-2 sps (two 3-dc groups along each of 4 sides between corner ch-2 sps).

Fasten off.

Rnd 3 From RS, join 3rd yarn color with a sl st in any corner ch-2 sp, ch 3 (counts as dc), 2 dc in same corner ch-2 sp, 3 dc in next sp between 3-dc groups, *(3 dc, ch 2, 3 dc) in next corner ch-2 sp, 3 dc in next sp between 3-dc groups; rep from * 2 more times, 3 dc again in first corner ch-2 sp, ch 2; join with sl st in top of beg ch-3—36 dc and 4 corner ch-2 sps (three 3-dc groups along each of 4 sides between corner ch-2 sps).

Fasten off.

Rnd 4 From RS, join 4th yarn color with a sl st in any corner ch-2 sp, ch 3 (counts as dc), 2 dc in same corner ch-2 sp, 3 dc in each sp between 3-dc groups to next corner ch-2 sp, *(3 dc, ch 2, 3 dc) in next corner ch-2 sp, 3 dc in each sp between 3-dc groups to next corner ch-2 sp; rep from * 2 more times, 3 dc again in first corner ch-2 sp, ch 2; join with sl st in top of beg ch-3—48 dc and 4 corner ch-2 sps (four 3-dc groups along each of 4 sides between corner ch-2 sps).

Fasten off.

Rnd 5 With A, rep Rnd 4—60 dc and 4 corner ch-2 sps (five 3-dc groups along each of 4 sides between corner ch-2 sps).

Fasten off, leaving a long yarn tail for sewing.

FINISHING

Lay Squares out into 9 rows of 12 Squares each. Sew Squares together. The easiest way to sew the Squares together is to sew 9 strips of 12 Squares each, then sew the strips together.

Border

From RS, join A with a sl st on outside edge of Afghan. Work sc evenly spaced around outside edge, working 3 sc in each corner; join with sl st in first sc.

Fasten off.

Weave in ends. •

KEY
- • = slip stitch (sl st)
- ○ = chain (ch)
- ┬ = double crochet (dc)

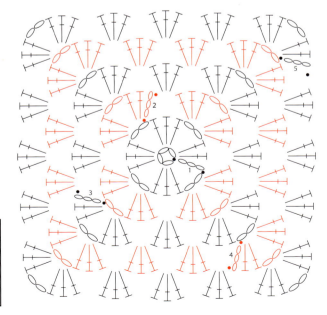

Granny Square Scarf & Earflap Hat

Easy

MEASUREMENTS
HAT
Finished Circumference Approx 17½"/44.5cm, will stretch to fit a range of sizes
Finished Height Approx 8"/20.5cm
SCARF
Approx 7 x 48"/18 x 122cm

MATERIALS
YARN
LION BRAND® Heartland®, 5oz/142g balls, each approx 251yd/230m (acrylic/rayon)
- 1 ball each in #153 Black Canyon (A) and #098 Acadia (B)

HOOK
- Size I-9 (5.5mm) crochet hook, *or size to obtain gauge*

NOTIONS
- Tapestry needle
- 2 x 4"/5 x 10cm piece of cardboard

GAUGE
One Square = approx 3½"/9cm square.
BE SURE TO CHECK YOUR GAUGE.

STITCH GLOSARY
FPTR (front post treble crochet) Yarn over twice, insert hook from front to back then to front, going around post of indicated st, draw up a loop, (yarn over and draw through 2 loops on hook) 3 times. Skip st behind the FPTR.

NOTES
1) Hat is made from 13 pieces: 10 Squares, 1 Pentagon Motif, and 2 Earflaps. All pieces are sewn together to make the Hat.
2) Scarf is made from 18 Squares sewn together following the Assembly Diagram.

HAT
SQUARE I (MAKE 5)
With A, ch 4; join with sl st in first ch to form a ring.
Rnd 1 (RS) Ch 3 (counts as dc in this rnd and all following rnds), 2 dc in ring, [ch 2, 3 dc in ring] 3 times, ch 2; join with sl st in top of beg ch—4 ch-2 sps and 12 dc (four 3-dc groups). Fasten off.
Rnd 2 From RS, draw up a loop of B in any ch-2 sp, ch 3, (dc, ch 2, 2 dc) in same ch-2 sp, *dc in each st to next ch-2 sp, (2 dc, ch 2, 2 dc) in next ch-2 sp (corner made); rep from * 2 more times, dc in each st around; join with sl st in top of beg ch—4 ch-2 sps and 28 dc (7 dc across each edge between corner ch-2 sps). Fasten off.
Rnd 3 From RS, draw up a loop of A in any ch-2 sp, ch 3, (dc, ch 2, 2 dc) in same ch-sp, *dc in next 3 sts, FPTR around center dc of 3-dc group of Rnd 1, dc in next 3 sts, (2 dc, ch 2, 2 dc) in next ch-2 sp; rep from * 2 more times, dc in next 3 sts, FPTR around center dc of 3-dc group of Rnd 1, dc in next 3 sts; join with sl st in top of beg ch—4 ch-2 sps and 44 sts (11 sts across each edge between corner ch-2 sps). Fasten off.

SQUARE II (MAKE 5)
Make same as Square I, working Rnd 1 with B, Rnd 2 with A, and Rnd 3 with B.

PENTAGON MOTIF
With B, ch 4; join with sl st in first ch to form a ring.
Rnd 1 (RS) Ch 3 (counts as dc in this rnd and all following rnds), 2 dc in ring, [ch 2, 3 dc in ring] 4 times, ch 2; join

with sl st in top of beg ch—5 ch-2 sps and 15 dc (five 3-dc groups). Fasten off.

Rnd 2 From RS, draw up a loop of A in any ch-2 sp, ch 3, (dc, ch 2, 2 dc) in same ch-2 sp, *dc in each st to next ch-2 sp, (2 dc, ch 2, 2 dc) in next ch-2 sp (corner made); rep from * 3 more times, dc in each st to end of rnd; join with sl st in top of beg ch—4 ch-2 sps and 35 dc (7 dc across each edge between corner ch-2 sps). Fasten off.

Rnd 3 From RS, draw up a loop of B in any ch-2 sp, ch 3, (dc, ch 2, 2 dc) in same ch-sp, *dc in next 3 sts, FPTR around center dc of 3-dc group of Rnd 1, dc in next 3 sts, (2 dc, ch 2, 2 dc) in next ch-2 sp; rep from * 3 more times, dc in next 3 sts, FPTR around center dc of 3-dc group of Rnd 1, dc in next 3 sts; join with sl st in top of beg ch—4 ch-2 sps and 55 sts (11 sts across each edge between corner ch-2 sps). Fasten off.

EARFLAPS (MAKE 2)

Note To change color while working earflaps, work last st of old color to last yarn over. Yarn over with new color and draw through all loops on hook to complete st. Fasten off old color. Proceed with new color.

With A, ch 3; join with sl st in first ch to form a ring.

Row 1 Ch 5 (counts as dc, ch 2 in this row and all following rows), [3 dc in ring, ch 2] twice, dc in ring and change to B—3 ch-2 sps and 8 dc (two 3-dc groups and a dc at beg and end of row).

Row 2 With B, ch 5, turn, 2 dc in first ch-2 sp, dc in next 3 dc, (2 dc, ch 2, 2 dc) in next ch-2 sp, dc in next 3 dc, (2 dc, ch 2, dc) in last ch-2 sp and change to A—3 ch-2 sps and 16 dc.

Granny Square Scarf & Earflap Hat

Row 3 With A, ch 3 (counts as dc), turn, 2 dc in first ch-2 sp, dc in next 3 dc, FPTR around center dc of 3-dc group of Row 1, dc in next 3 dc, (2 dc, ch 2, 2 dc) in next ch-2 sp, dc in next 3 dc, FPTR around center dc of 3-dc group of Row 1, dc in next 3 dc, 3 dc in last ch-2 sp—1 ch-2 sp and 24 sts. Do not change color.
Row 4 With A, ch 1, turn, work 10 sc evenly spaced across to ch-2 sp, 4 sc in ch-2 sp, work 10 sc evenly spaced across to end of row.
Fasten off.

HAT FINISHING

Sew all 5 Square I's into a strip. Rep with all 5 Square II's. Sew one long edge of strips tog to make a rectangle. Sew short ends of rectangle tog to make a tube.
Sew edges of Pentagon Motif to open edge of Square II strip for top of Hat.
Sew straight edge of one Earflap to lower edge of Hat, beg at center of one Square and ending at center of next Square.
Sew straight edge of 2nd Earflap to lower edge of Hat, beg at center of next Square following first Earflap. The 2 halves of Squares skipped between Earflaps are at back of Hat.

EARFLAP TIES

From RS, join 2 strands of A held tog with sl st in tip of one Earflap, ch 40. Fasten off. Rep for tie on 2nd Earflap.

TASSELS (MAKE 2)

Wrap A and B around 2"/5cm side of cardboard 20 times. Cut a 6"/15cm length of A and thread doubled into tapestry needle. Insert needle under all strands at upper edge of cardboard. Pull tightly and knot securely near strands. Cut yarn loops at lower edge of cardboard. Cut a 12"/30.5cm length of A and wrap tightly around loops 1½"/4cm below top knot to form Tassel neck. Knot securely; thread ends onto needle and weave ends to center of Tassel. Trim Tassel ends evenly.
Tie one tassel to end of each Earflap tie.

SCARF

SQUARE I (MAKE 9)
Make same as Square I of Hat.

SQUARE II (MAKE 9)
Make same as Square II of Hat.

SCARF FINISHING

Folllowing Assembly Diagram, sew Squares together into pairs and then into a strip.
Weave in ends. •

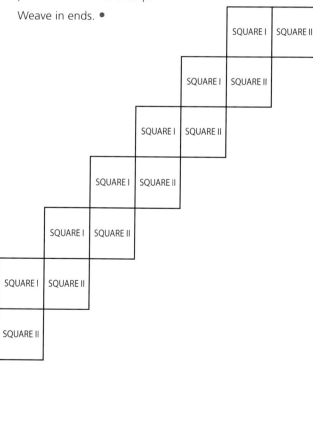

Granny Square Dog Sweater

Easy

SIZES
S (M, L, XL).

MEASUREMENTS
Finished Chest 11¼ (19½, 25½, 30½)"/28.5 (49.5, 65, 77.5)cm
Finished Length 10½ (17, 22½, 27½)"/26.5 (43, 57, 70)cm

MATERIALS
YARN
LION BRAND® Wool-Ease® Thick & Quick®, 6oz/170g balls, each approx 106yd/97m (acrylic/wool)
- 1 (1, 2, 3) balls in #132 Lemongrass

HOOK
- Size P-15 (10mm) crochet hook, *or size to obtain gauge*

NOTIONS
- Tapestry needle

GAUGE
6 hdc + 5 rows = 4"/10cm.
BE SURE TO CHECK YOUR GAUGE.

DOG SWEATER
BACK
Ch 4; join with sl st in first ch to form a ring.
Rnd 1 Ch 2 (counts as hdc), hdc in ring, *ch 2, 2 hdc in ring; rep from * 2 more times, ch 2; join with sl st in top of beg ch.
Rnd 2 Sl st to first ch-2 sp, ch 2 (counts as hdc here and throughout), hdc in same ch-2 sp, *ch 2, 2 hdc in same ch-2 sp, ch 1, 2 hdc in next ch-2 sp; rep from * 2 more times, ch 2, 2 hdc in same ch-2 sp, ch 1; join with sl st in top of beg ch.
Rnd 3 Sl st to first ch-2 sp, ch 2, hdc in same ch-2 sp, *ch 2, 2 hdc in same ch-2 sp, [ch 1, 2 hdc in next ch-sp] 2 times; rep from * 2 more times, ch 2, 2 hdc in same ch-2 sp, ch 1, 2 hdc in next ch-sp, ch 1; join with sl st in top of beg ch.
Rnd 4 Sl st to first ch-2 sp, ch 2, hdc in same ch-2 sp, *ch 2, 2 hdc in same ch-2 sp, ch 1, [2 hdc in next ch-sp, ch1] across to next ch-2 sp, 2 hdc in ch-2 sp; rep from * 2 more times, ch 2, 2 hdc in same ch-2 sp, [ch 1, 2 hdc in next ch-sp] across to beg ch, ch 1; join with sl st in top of beg ch.
Rep last rnd 1 (4, 7, 9) times. Fasten off.

Granny Square Dog Sweater

UNDERPIECE

Work as for Back for 2 (4, 5, 6) rnds. Do not fasten off.

Neck

Sl st to first ch-2 sp.

Rnd 1 Ch 2, hdc in each hdc and ch-sp on one edge of Underpiece, hdc in each hdc and ch-sp along one edge of Back; join with sl st in top of beg ch.

Rnd 2 Ch 2, hdc in each hdc around; join with sl st in top of beg ch.

Rep last rnd 1 (3, 4, 6) more times.

Fasten off.

FINISHING

Sew sides of Underpiece to Back, leaving 2 (2½, 3, 3½)"/ 5 (6.5, 7.5, 9)cm open on each side for legs.

Weave in ends. •

BACK

6½ (13, 17½, 21) in.

6½ (13, 17½, 21) in.

UNDERPIECE

3¼ (6½, 8, 9½) in.

3¼ (6½, 8, 9½) in.

Multi-Granny Square Market Bag

Easy

MEASUREMENTS
Finished Width 13½"/34.5cm
Finished Height (excluding straps) 16"/40.5cm

MATERIALS

YARN
LION BRAND® Wool-Ease®, 3oz/85g balls, each approx 197yd/180m (acrylic/wool)
- 1 ball each in #099 Fishermen (A), #151 Grey Heather (B), #114 Denim (C), #140 Rose Heather (D), #138 Cranberry (E), and #180 Forest Green Heather (F)

HOOK
- Size I-9 (5.5mm) crochet hook, *or size to obtain gauge*

NOTIONS
- Tapestry needle

GAUGE
1 Granny Square = approx 4½"/11.5cm square.
BE SURE TO CHECK YOUR GAUGE.

NOTES
1) Market Bag is made from 18 Granny Squares worked separately and then sewn together.
2) Each Granny Square is worked in joined rounds, changing yarn color following color sequences.
3) Top edging and handles are worked directly onto top of Bag.

COLOR SEQUENCES

COLOR SEQUENCE I
Work 1 rnd with A, 1 rnd with D, 1 rnd with E, and 1 rnd with A.

COLOR SEQUENCE II
Work 1 rnd with D, 1 rnd with A, 1 rnd with C, and 1 rnd with A.

COLOR SEQUENCE III
Work 1 rnd with E, 1 rnd with C, 1 rnd with B, and 1 rnd with A.

COLOR SEQUENCE IV
Work 1 rnd with C, 1 rnd with F, 1 rnd with B, and 1 rnd with A.

COLOR SEQUENCE V
Work 1 rnd with F, 1 rnd with B, 1 rnd with D, and 1 rnd with A.

Multi-Granny Square Market Bag

COLOR SEQUENCE VI
Work 1 rnd with F, 1 rnd with D, 1 rnd with C, and 1 rnd with A.

COLOR SEQUENCE VII
Work 1 rnd with B, 1 rnd with E, 1 rnd with F, and 1 rnd with A.

COLOR SEQUENCE VIII
Work 1 rnd with A, 1 rnd with B, 1 rnd with E, and 1 rnd with A.

COLOR SEQUENCE IX
Work 1 rnd with E, 1 rnd with C, 1 rnd with D, and 1 rnd with A.

BAG

GRANNY SQUARES (MAKE 18—2 EACH IN COLOR SEQUENCES I–IX)
With first color, ch 4.

Rnd 1 (RS) With first color, 2 dc in 3rd ch from hook (3 skipped ch count as dc), [ch 2, 3 dc in same ch] 3 times; join with sl st in top of beg ch—you will have four 3-dc groups and 4 ch-2 sps in this rnd.
Fasten off.

Rnd 2 From RS, draw up a loop of 2nd color in any ch-2 sp, ch 3 (counts as dc), 2 dc in same ch-2 sp, *ch 2, (3 dc, ch 2, 3 dc) in next ch-2 sp (corner made); rep from * 2 more times, ch 2, 3 dc in first ch-2 sp, ch 2 (first corner completed); join with sl st in top of beg ch-3—eight 3-dc groups and 8 ch-2 sps (two 3-dc groups and 1 ch-2 sp along each of 4 sides between corner ch-2 sps).
Fasten off.

Rnd 3 From RS, draw up a loop of 3rd color in any corner ch-2 sp, ch 3 (counts as dc), 2 dc in same ch-2 sp, *ch 2, 3 dc in next ch-2 sp, ch 2, (3 dc, ch 2, 3 dc) in next corner ch-2 sp; rep from * 2 more times, ch 2, 3 dc in next ch-2 sp, ch 2, 3 dc in first ch-2 sp, ch 2; join with sl st in top of beg ch-3—twelve 3-dc groups and 12 ch-2 sps (three 3-dc groups and 2 ch-2 sp along each of 4 sides between corner ch-2 sps).
Fasten off.

Rnd 4 From RS, draw up a loop of fourth color in any corner ch-2 sp, ch 3 (counts as dc), 2 dc in same ch-2 sp, *[ch 2, 3 dc in next ch-2 sp] twice, ch 2, (3 dc, ch 2, 3 dc) in next corner ch-2 sp; rep from * 2 more times, [ch 2, 3 dc in next ch-2 sp] twice, ch 2, 3 dc in first ch-2 sp, ch 2; join with sl st in top of beg ch-3—sixteen 3-dc groups and 16 ch-2 sps (four 3-dc groups and 3 ch-2 sp along each of 4 sides between corner ch-2 sps).
Fasten off.

FINISHING
Weave in ends. Block each Granny Square to 4½"/11.5cm square.
Sew Granny Squares into 3 strips of 6 Granny Squares each, placing colors as desired.
Sew strips tog to form a rectangle, 3 Squares x 6 Squares. Fold rectangle in half, so that front and back are each 3 Squares x 3 Squares. Sew sides, leaving top open.

Top Edging and Handles
From RS, draw up a loop of A in top of either side seam.

Rnd 1 Ch 3 (counts as dc), work 50 dc sts evenly spaced along top edge of front then 51 dc sts evenly spaced along top edge of back; join with sl st in top of beg ch-3—102 dc.

Rnd 2 Ch 3 (counts as dc), dc in each st around; join with sl st in top of beg ch-3.

Rnd 3 Ch 3 (counts as dc), dc in next 16 sts, ch 60, sk next 17 sts (for first handle), dc in next 34 sts, ch 60, sk next 17 sts (for 2nd handle), dc in last 17 sts; join with sl st in top of beg ch-3—68 dc and 2 ch-60 handles.

Rnd 4 Ch 3 (counts as dc), dc in next 16 sts, sc in next 60 ch, dc in next 34 sts, sc in next 60 ch, dc in last 17 sts; join with sl st in top of beg ch-3—188 sts.

Rnd 5 Ch 3 (counts as dc), dc in next 16 sts, sc in next 60 sts, dc in next 34 sts, sc in next 60 sts, dc in last 17 sts; join with sl st in top of beg ch-3.
Fasten off.

Weave in ends. •

Granny Square Sweater

Easy

SIZES
XS/S (M/L, 1X/2X/3X, 4X/5X).

MEASUREMENTS
Finished Bust Approx 36 (44, 54, 66)"/91.5 (112, 137, 167.5)cm
Finished Length (including lower edging) 20 (24, 24½, 29½)"/51 (61, 62, 75)cm

MATERIALS
YARN
LION BRAND® Wool-Ease®, 3oz/85g balls, each approx 197yd/180m (acrylic/wool)
- 4 (4, 5, 5) balls in #099 Fishermen (A)
- 1 ball each in #151 Grey Heather (B), #114 Denim (C), #140 Rose Heather (D), #138 Cranberry (E), and #180 Forest Green Heather (F)

HOOK
For sizes XS/S and 1X/2X/3X only
- Size I-9 (5.5mm) crochet hook, *or size to obtain gauge*

For sizes M/L and 4X/5X only
- Size K-10.5 (6.5mm) crohet hook, *or size to obtain gauge*

NOTIONS
- Tapestry needle

GAUGE
For sizes XS/S and 1X/2X/3X only
1 Square = approx 4½"/11.5cm.
For sizes M/L and 4X/5X only
1 Square = approx 5½"/14cm.
BE SURE TO CHECK YOUR GAUGE.

NOTES
1) Sweater is made from 38 (38, 70, 70) Granny Squares.
2) Size of Squares is achieved by using different size hooks.
3) Granny Squares are worked in joined rounds with Right Side facing. Yarn color is changed every round. Fasten off old color and join new color, as instructed.
4) The Squares are sewn together following a diagram to make the Sweater.
5) When sewing Squares together, place colors as desired. Designer suggests mirroring sleeves and fronts.
6) An edging is worked around wrists and along outside edge of Sweater.

SWEATER
GRANNY SQUARES
Make Granny Squares in the following color combinations, listed from Rnd 1 to Rnd 4.
Note Be sure to use the specific size hook indicated for your size Sweater.

Square 1 – make 6 (6, 9, 9): A, D, E, A
Square 2 – make 5 (5, 9, 9): D, A, C, A
Square 3 – make 5 (5, 9, 9): E, C, B, A
Square 4 – make 5 (5, 9, 9): C, F, B, A
Square 5 – make 5 (5, 9, 9): F, B, D, A
Square 6 – make 5 (5, 9, 9): F, D, C, A
Square 7 – make 4 (4, 8, 8): B, E, F, A
Square 8 – make 3 (3, 8, 8): A, B, E, A

Rnd 1 (RS) With first color, ch 3, 2 dc in 3rd ch from hook (2 skipped ch count as dc), *ch 2, 3 dc in same ch; rep from * 2 more times, ch 2: join with sl st in top of beg ch-2—you will have 12 dc and 4 ch-2 sps in this rnd (four 3-dc groups and 4 ch-2 sps).
Fasten off.

Granny Square Sweater

Rnd 2 With 2nd color, make slipknot and place it on hook. From RS, 3 dc in any ch-2 sp, *ch 2, (3 dc, ch 2, 3 dc) in next ch-2 sp (corner made); rep from * 2 more times, ch 2, 3 dc again in first ch-2 sp, ch 2; join with sl st in first dc—eight 3-dc groups, 4 corner ch-2 sps, and 4 side ch-2 sps.
Fasten off.

Rnd 3 With 3rd color, make a slipknot and place it on hook. From RS, 3 dc in any corner ch-2 sp, *ch 2, 3 dc in next ch-2 sp, ch 2, (3 dc, ch 2, 3 dc) in next corner ch-2 sp; rep from * 2 more times, ch 2, 3 dc in next ch-2 sp, ch 2, 3 dc again in first corner ch-2 sp, ch 2; join with sl st in first dc—twelve 3-dc groups, 4 corner ch-2 sps, and 8 side ch-2 sps.
Fasten off.

Rnd 4 With 4th color, make a slipknot and place it on hook. From RS, 3 dc in any corner ch-2 sp, *ch 2, [3 dc in next ch-2 sp, ch 2] twice, (3 dc, ch 2, 3 dc) in next corner ch-2 sp; rep from * 2 more times, ch 2, [3 dc in next ch-2 sp, ch 2] twice, 3 dc again in first corner ch-2 sp, ch 2; join with sl st in first dc—sixteen 3-dc groups, 4 corner ch-2 sps, and 12 side ch-2 sps.
Fasten off.

FINISHING

Weave in ends.
Block Squares to size, then sew tog following diagram.
Sew side and sleeve seams.

SLEEVE EDGING

Rnd 1 From RS, draw up a loop of A in corner ch-2 sp at back of wrist edge, ch 2 (counts as dc), dc evenly spaced around; join with sl st in first dc.
Rnds 2–4 Ch 2 (counts as dc), dc in each st around; join with sl st in top of beg ch-2.
Note To shape Sleeve, work Rnd 5 tightly.
Rnd 5 Sl st in each st around.
Fasten off.
Rep to work edging around edge of 2nd sleeve.

LOWER EDGING

Rnd 1 From RS, draw up a loop of A in lower front corner so that you are ready to work along lower edge of Sweater.
Ch 3 (counts as dc), dc evenly spaced along lower edge.
Rows 2–4 Ch 2 (counts as dc), turn, dc in each st across.
Fasten off.

FRONT EDGING

Rnd 1 From RS, draw up a loop of A in lower front corner so that you are ready to work along front edge of Sweater.
Working in ends of rows, dc evenly spaced up side edge of lower edging and front edge of Sweater, across back neck, and down opposite front edge and side edge of lower edging.
Rows 2–12 Ch 2 (counts as dc), turn, dc in each st across.
Fasten off.

Weave in ends. •

SCHEMATIC FOR XS/S (M/L)

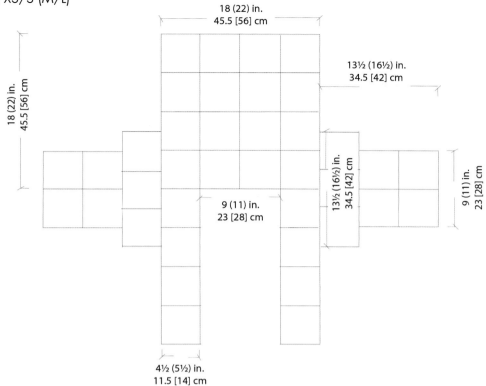

SCHEMATIC FOR 1X/2X/3X (4X/5X)

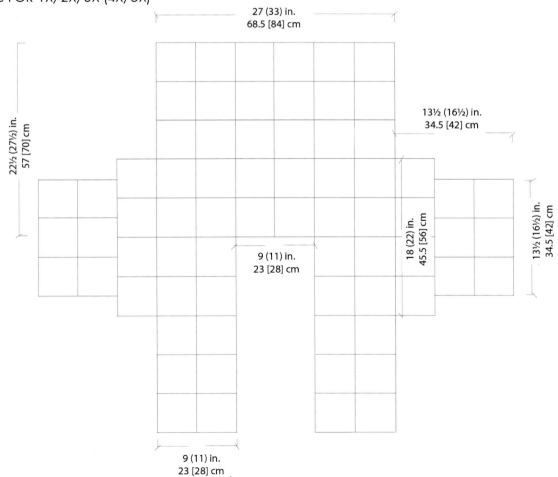

Granny Triangle Scarf

Easy

MEASUREMENTS
Approx 6 x 60"/15 x 152.5cm, including border

MATERIALS
YARN
LION BRAND® Heartland®, 5oz/142g balls, each approx 251yd/230m (acrylic/rayon)
• 1 ball each in #153 Black Canyon (A), #122 Grand Canyon (B), and #147 Hot Springs (C)

HOOK
• Size I-9 (5.5mm) crochet hook, or size to obtain gauge

NOTIONS
• Tapestry needle

GAUGE
One Triangle = approx 6½"/16.5cm measured across one side.
BE SURE TO CHECK YOUR GAUGE.

STITCH GLOSSARY
triangle-join Drop loop from hook, insert hook from RS to WS through corresponding ch-sp of previous Triangle and return the dropped loop to the hook, draw the loop through the ch-sp.

NOTES
1) Scarf is made from 17 Triangles joined together into a strip. Triangle 1 is worked first, then remaining Triangles are worked using a join-as-you-go technique while working the last round of each Triangle.
2) Triangles are worked in joined rounds with RS always facing.
3) Color is changed on every other round by fastening off old color and joining the new color as instructed.

SCARF
TRIANGLE 1
With C, ch 4; join with sl st in first ch to form a ring.
Rnd 1 (RS) Ch 1, sc in ring, [ch 3, sc in ring] 5 times, ch 3; join with sl st in first sc—6 sc and 6 ch-3 sps at the end of this rnd.
Rnd 2 (Sl st, ch 1, sc, ch 3, sc) in first ch-3 sp, *ch 3, (sc, ch 3, sc) in next ch-3 sp; rep from * 4 more times, ch 3; join with sl st in first sc—12 sc and 12 ch-3 sps. Fasten off.
Rnd 3 (RS) From RS, join B with a sc in any ch-3 sp of Rnd 2, [ch 1, sc in next ch-3 sp] twice, *ch 1, (2 dc, ch 3, 2 dc) in next ch-3 sp (corner made)**, [ch 1, sc in next ch-3 sp] 3 times; rep from * once more, then from * to **, ch 1; join with sl st in first sc—3 corners, 9 sc, and 12 ch-1 sps.
Rnd 4 (Sl st, ch 1, sc) in first ch-1 sp, [ch 1, sc in next ch-1 sp] twice, *ch 1, sk next dc, sc in next dc, (sc, ch 3, sc) in next ch-3 sp, sc in next dc, ch 1, sk next dc, sc in next ch-1 sp **, [ch 1, sc in next ch-1 sp] 3 times; rep from * once more, then from * to **, ch 1; join with sl st in first sc—24 sc, 15 ch-1 sps, and 3 corner ch-3 sps. Fasten off.
Rnd 5 (RS) From RS, join A with a sc in any sc immediately before a corner ch-3 sp, ch 2, sc in same sc, *(sc, ch 2, sc, ch 6, sc, ch 2, sc) in corner ch-3 sp, (sc, ch 2, sc) in next sc, (sc, ch 2, sc) in each of next 5 ch-1 sps, sk next sc **, (sc, ch 2, sc) in next sc; rep from * once more, then from * to **; join with sl st in first sc. Fasten off.

TRIANGLES 2–17
Rnds 1–4 Work same as Rnds 1–4 of Triangle 1.
Notes On Rnd 5, the current Triangle is completed and

Granny Triangle Scarf

joined to previous Triangle across one edge, from corner to corner. Be sure to read through the explanation for triangle-join in the Stitch Explanation section before beginning.

Rnd 5 (Joining Rnd):

Complete first edge: From RS, join A with a sc in any sc immediately before a corner ch-3 sp, ch 2, sc in same sc, (sc, ch 2, sc, ch 6, sc, ch 2, sc) in corner ch-3 sp, (sc, ch 2, sc) in next sc, (sc, ch 2, sc) in each of next 5 ch-1 sps, sk next sc, (sc, ch 2, sc) in next sc.

Join next edge to previous Triangle: Hold current Triangle and previous Triangle with WS tog and sts matching. Take care that next edge to be worked will join current Triangle to form a strip (not a curve): (sc, ch 2, sc, ch 3, triangle-join, ch 3, sc, ch 1, triangle-join, ch 1, sc) in corner ch-3 sp, (sc, ch 1, triangle-join, ch 1, sc) in next sc, (sc, ch 1, triangle-join, ch 1, sc) in each of next 5 ch-1 sps, sk next sc, (sc, ch 1, triangle-join, ch 1, sc) in next sc, (sc, ch 1, triangle-join, ch 1, sc, ch 3, triangle-join, ch 3, sc, ch 2, sc) in corner ch-3 sp.

Complete last edge: (sc, ch 2, sc) in next sc, (sc, ch 2, sc) in each of next 5 ch-1 sps, sk next sc; join with sl st in first sc.

Fasten off.

FINISHING

BORDER

Rnd 1 (RS) From RS, join A with a sc in any ch-2 sp near center of either long edge of Scarf, ch 2, sc in same ch-2 sp, (sc, ch 2, sc) in each ch-2 sp, working (sc, ch 3, sc) in each corner sp between Triangles and (sc, ch 2, sc, ch 3, sc, ch 2, sc) in ch-6 sp at each end of Scarf; join with sl st in first sc.

Fasten off.

Weave in ends. •

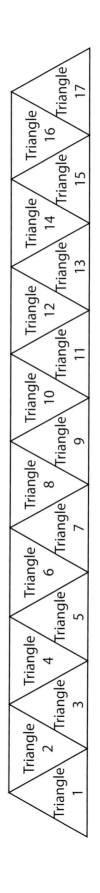

Sparkly Granny Hat

Easy

MEASUREMENTS
Finished Circumference Approx 19"/48.5cm, will stretch to fit a range of sizes

MATERIALS
YARN
LION BRAND® Bonbons®, 2⁴/₅oz/80g total, approx 224yd/208m (acrylic/other)
- 1 package in #660 Celebrate

Colors: Dark Blue (A), Sparkling Peach (B), Emerald (C), Pea Green (D), Hot Pink (E), Red (F), Light Blue (G), and Purple (H)

HOOK
- Size G-6 (4.25mm) crochet hook, *or size to obtain gauge*

NOTIONS
- Tapestry needle

GAUGE
Square 1 = 3¼"/8.5cm.
BE SURE TO CHECK YOUR GAUGE.

NOTES
1) 6 Squares are made, then sewed together to make a ring.
2) Top of Hat is worked around top of joined Squares.
3) The color is changed on every round of each Square. Change color by fastening off old color and drawing up a loop of new color in a corner ch-2 space.

HAT
SQUARE I (MAKE 1)
With A, ch 6; join with sl st in first ch to form a ring.
Rnd 1 (RS) Ch 3 (counts as dc in this rnd and in all following rnds), 2 dc in ring, [ch 2, 3 dc in ring] 3 times, ch 2; join with sl st in top of beg ch—12 dc and 4 ch-2 sps. Fasten off.
Rnd 2 From RS, draw up a loop of B in any ch-2 sp, ch 3, (2 dc, ch 2, 3 dc) in same ch-2 sp (first corner made), *ch 1, (3 dc, ch 2, 3 dc) in next ch-2 sp (corner made); rep from * 2 more times, ch 1; join with sl st in top of beg ch—24 dc and 4 corner ch-2 sps. Fasten off.
Rnd 3 From RS, draw up a loop of C in any ch-2 sp, ch 3, (2 dc, ch 2, 3 dc) in same ch-2 sp, *ch 1, 3 dc in next ch-1 sp, ch 1, (3 dc, ch 2, 3 dc) in next ch-2 sp; rep from * 2 more times, ch 1, 3 dc in next ch-1 sp, ch 1; join with sl st in top of beg ch—36 dc and 4 corner ch-2 sps. Fasten off.

Sparkly Granny Hat

Rnd 4 From RS draw up a loop of D in any ch-2 sp, ch 3, (2 dc, ch 2, 3 dc) in same ch-2 sp, *[ch 1, 3 dc in next ch-1 sp] twice, ch 1, (3 dc, ch 2, 3 dc) in next ch-2 sp; rep from * 2 more times, [ch 1, 3 dc in next ch-1 sp] twice, ch 1; join with sl st in top of beg ch—48 dc and 4 corner ch-2 sps. Fasten off.

SQUARE II (MAKE 2)
Same as Square I but work 1 rnd each with D, C, B, A.

SQUARE III (MAKE 2)
Same as Square I but work 1 rnd each with H, G, F, E.

SQUARE IV (MAKE 1)
Same as Square I but work 1 rnd each with E, F, G, H.

Sew Squares into a strip in the following order: Square II, Square III, Square I, Square IV, Square II, Square III. Sew first and last Squares tog to make a ring.

CROWN
Draw up a loop of F in any ch-1 sp on one edge of ring.
Rnd 1 (RS) Ch 3 (counts as dc in this rnd and in all following rnds), 2 dc in same ch-sp, *ch 1, 3 dc in next ch-1 sp or next join between Squares (do not work into the corner ch-2 sps of the Squares); rep from * around, ch 1; join with sl st in top of beg ch—twenty-four 3-dc groups. Fasten off.
Rnd 2 From RS, draw up a loop of G in any ch-1 sp, ch 3, 2 dc in same ch-1 sp, *ch 1, 3 dc in next ch-1 sp; rep from * around, ch 1; join with sl st in top of beg ch. Fasten off.
Rnd 3 With H, rep Rnd 2. Fasten off.
Rnd 4 With A, rep Rnd 2. Fasten off.
Rnd 5 From RS, draw up a loop of B in any ch-1 sp, ch 3, 2 dc in same ch-1 sp, [ch 1, 3 dc in next ch-1 sp] twice, ch 1, dc in next ch-1 sp, *[ch 1, 3 dc in next ch-1 sp] 3 times, ch 1, dc in next ch-1 sp; rep from * around, ch 1; join with sl st in top of beg ch—eighteen 3-dc groups and 6 dc. Fasten off.
Rnd 6 From RS, draw up a loop of C in any dc not part of a 3-dc group, ch 3, 2 dc in same dc, ch 1, sk next ch-1 sp, [3 dc in next ch-1 sp, ch 1] twice, *sk next ch-1 sp, 3 dc in next dc, ch 1, sk next ch-1 sp, [3 dc in next ch-1 sp, ch 1] twice; rep from * around; join with sl st in top of beg ch—eighteen 3-dc groups. Fasten off.
Rnd 7 From RS, draw up a loop of D in any ch-1 sp, ch 3, 2 dc in same ch-1 sp, ch 1, 3 dc in next ch-1 sp, ch 1, dc in next ch-1 sp, *[ch 1, 3 dc in next ch-1 sp] twice, ch 1, dc in next ch-1 sp; rep from * around, ch 1; join with sl st in top of beg ch—twelve 3-dc groups and 6 dc. Fasten off.
Rnd 8 From RS, draw up a loop of H in any dc not a part of a 3-dc group, ch 3, 2 dc in same dc, ch 1, sk next ch-1 sp, 3 dc in next ch-1 sp, *ch 1, sk next ch-1 sp, 3 dc in next dc, ch 1, sk next ch-1 sp, 3 dc in next ch-1 sp; rep from * around, ch 1; join with sl st in top of beg ch—twelve 3-dc groups. Fasten off.
Rnd 9 From RS, draw up a loop of G in any ch-1 sp, ch 3, 2 dc in same ch-1 sp, ch 1, dc in next ch-1 sp, *ch 1, 3 dc in next ch-1 sp, ch 1, dc in next ch-1 sp; rep from * around, ch 1; join with sl st in top of beg ch—six 3-dc groups and 6 dc. Fasten off.
Rnd 10 From RS, draw up a loop of F in any dc not a part of a 3-dc group, ch 3, 2 dc in same dc, ch 1, *sk next 2 ch-1 sps, 3 dc in next dc, ch 1; rep from * around, sk last 2 ch-1 sps; join with sl st in top of beg ch—six 3-dc groups. Fasten off.
Rnd 11 From RS, draw up a loop of E in any ch-1 sp, ch 4 (counts as dc, ch 1), *dc in next ch-1 sp, ch 1; rep from * around; join with sl st in 3rd ch of beg ch—6 dc. Fasten off, leaving a long yarn tail. Thread yarn tail through sts of last rnd and pull to gather. Knot securely.

LOWER EDGING
Working around opposite edge of ring of Squares, rep Rnds 1–3 of Crown. Fasten off.

FINISHING
Weave in ends. •

Silvery Granny Throw

Intermediate

MEASUREMENTS
Approx 48 x 64"/122 x 162.5cm

MATERIALS
YARN
LION BRAND® Vanna's Choice®, 3½oz/100g balls, each approx 170yd/156m (acrylic)
- 6 balls in #149 Silver Grey (A)
- 4 balls in #105 Silver Blue (B)
- 3 balls in #108 Dusty Blue (C)
- 2 balls in #405 Silver Heather (D)

HOOK
- Size J-10 (6mm) crochet hook, *or size to obtain gauge*

NOTIONS
- Tapestry needle

GAUGE
One Square = 5½"/14cm.
BE SURE TO CHECK YOUR GAUGE.

STITCH GLOSSARY
beg-dc Leaving a long tail to weave in later, hold the working yarn firmly against the hook, [yarn over] twice, insert hook in indicated st, yarn over and draw up a loop (3 loops on hook), [yarn over and draw through 2 loops on hook] twice.

large-shell Work 5 dc in indicated st or sp.

sc2tog (sc 2 sts together) [Insert hook in next st and draw up a loop] twice, yarn over and draw through all 3 loops on hook—1 st decreased.

small-shell Work 3 dc in indicated st or sp.

square-join Drop loop from hook, insert hook from RS to WS through the corresponding ch-sp of the neighboring Square, return the dropped loop to the hook and draw it through the ch-sp.

NOTES
1) Throw is made from 83 Squares joined together using a join-as-you-go technique while working the last round.
2) Refer to Assembly Diagram before working the last round of each Square to determine neighboring Squares to which the current Square is to be joined.
3) To keep this project small and portable for as long as possible, you may wish to make all 83 Squares through Rnd 3. Then work the last 2 rounds, joining the Squares together while working Rnd 5.
4) In Rnds 2 and 3 the yarn can be joined and the first dc worked traditionally, by drawing up a loop of yarn and working chain 3. Alternately, the yarn can be joined and the first dc worked at the same time by working a beg-dc as described in the Stitch Glossary section above. Border is worked in rows onto completed Throw.

THROW
SQUARE 1
With D, ch 4; join with sl st in first ch to form a ring.

Rnd 1 (RS) Ch 3 (counts as first dc in this rnd and in all following rnds), 2 dc in ring, [ch 2, 3 dc in ring] 3 times, ch 2; join with sl st in top of beg ch—12 dc (four 3-dc groups) and 4 ch-2 sps. Fasten off.

Rnd 2 From RS, draw up a loop of C in any ch-2 sp, ch 3, (2 dc, ch 2, 3 dc) in same ch-2 sp (first corner made), *ch 2, (3 dc, ch 3, 3 dc) in next ch-2 sp (corner made); rep from * 2 more times, ch 2; join with sl st in top of beg ch—24 dc (eight 3-dc groups), and 8 ch-2 sps (4 side ch-2 sps and 4 corner ch-2 sps). Fasten off.

Rnd 3 From RS, draw up a loop of B in any side ch-2 sp, ch 3, 2 dc in same ch-2 sp, ch 2, (3 dc, ch 3, 3 dc) in next ch-2 sp (corner), *ch 2, 3 dc in next ch-2 sp, ch 2, (3 dc,

Silvery Granny Throw

ch 2, 3 dc) in next ch-2 sp; rep from * 2 more times, ch 2; join with sl st in top of beg ch—36 dc (twelve 3-dc groups). Fasten off.

Rnd 4 From RS, join A with sc in any corner ch-2 sp, ch 2, sc in same corner ch-2 sp, ch 1, sk next dc, sc in next dc, [ch 1, sc in next ch-2 sp, ch 1, sk next dc, sc in next dc] twice, *ch 1, (sc, ch 2, sc) in next corner ch-2 sp, ch 1, sk next dc, sc in next dc, [ch 1, sc in next ch-2 sp, ch 1, sk next dc, sc in next dc] twice; rep from * 2 more times, ch 1; join with sl st in first sc—28 sc, 24 ch-1 sps, and 4 corner ch-2 sps. Do not fasten off.

Rnd 5 With A, (sl st, ch 1, sc, ch 4, sc) in first corner ch-2 sp, *(sc, ch 2, sc) in each ch-1 sp across to next corner ch-2 sp, (sc, ch 4, sc) in next corner ch-2 sp; rep from * 2 more times, (sc, ch 2, sc) in each ch-1 sp to end of rnd; join with sl st in first sc—56 sc, 24 ch-2 sps, and 4 corner ch-4 sps. Fasten off.

SQUARES 2–83

With D, ch 4; join with sl st in first ch to form a ring.
Rnds 1–4 Work same as Rnds 1–4 of Square 1—28 sc, 24 ch-1 sps, and 4 corner ch-2 sps at the end of Rnd 4.
Notes
1) Each Square is joined to neighboring Square(s) across one or more side edge(s). The ch-2 sps across the side edge and the ch-4 sps at the beg and end of the side are joined as Rnd 5 is worked. Ch-sps are joined by carefully threading the ch of the current Square through the corresponding ch-sp of the neighboring Square. Read the instructions for "square-join" in the Stitch Glossary carefully before beginning.

2) Refer to Assembly Diagram for placement. Note the number of neighboring Squares to which the current Square needs to be joined. If you join Squares in the order indicated in the Assembly Diagram each Square will need to be joined to at most 2 neighboring Squares.

3) If the current Square needs to be joined to only one neighboring Square, work Rnd 5 (join one side). If the current Square needs to be joined to two neighboring Squares work Rnd 5 (join 2 sides).

4) When joining, hold the current Square and the neighboring Square with WS together, sts matching, and RS of current Square facing you.

Rnd 5 (join one side) With A, (sl st, ch 1, sc, ch 4, sc) in first corner ch-2 sp, (sc, ch 2, sc) in each ch-1 sp across to next corner ch-2 sp, (sc, ch 2, square-join, ch 2, sc) in next corner ch-2 sp, (sc, ch 1, square-join, ch 1, sc) in each ch-1 sp across to next corner ch-2 sp, (sc, ch 2, square-join, ch 2, sc) in next corner ch-2 sp, (sc, ch 2, sc) in each ch-1 sp across to next corner ch-2 sp, (sc, ch 4, sc) in next corner ch-2 sp, (sc, ch 2, sc) in each ch-1 sp to end of rnd; join with sl st in first sc. Fasten off.

Rnd 5 (join 2 sides) With A, (sl st, ch 1, sc, ch 4, sc) in first corner ch-2 sp, (sc, ch 2, sc) in each ch-1 sp across to next corner ch-2 sp, (sc, ch 2, square-join, ch 2, sc) in next corner ch-2 sp, *(sc, ch 1, square-join, ch 1, sc) in each ch-1 sp across to next corner ch-2 sp, (sc, ch 2, square-join, ch 2, sc) in next corner ch-2 sp; rep from * once more, (sc, ch 2, sc) in each ch-1 sp to end of rnd; join with sl st in first sc. Fasten off.

FINISHING
BORDER

Rnd 1 (RS) From RS, join A with sc in any ch-2 sp immediately following an outer/un-joined corner ch-4 sp, *small-shell in next ch-2 sp, sc in next ch-2 sp; rep from * around working in corner sps and 4 corner edges as follows:

Outer corners: Large-shell in each outer/un-joined corner ch-4 sp.

Inner corners: One sc in each ch-sp on each side of the square-join. **Note** This means that at inner corners you will work a small-shell in the ch-2 sp before the inner corner, two sc sts (one in the corner ch-sp on each side of the square-join) and then a small-shell in the following ch-2 sp.

Corner edges (un-joined edges of Squares 1, 26, 58, and 83 that form corners of Throw): Work large-shell in first corner ch-4 sp, sc in next ch-2 sp, small-shell in next ch-2 sp, sc in next ch-2 sp, small-shell in sp between next 2 sc, sc in next ch-2 sp, small-shell in next ch-2 sp, sc in next ch-2 sp, lg-shell in next corner ch-4 sp. **Note** This ensures that shells are alternated with sc sts all the way around. Join with sl st in first sc. Fasten off.

Rnd 2 From RS, join C with sc in same st as joining, *(sc, ch 2, sc) in center dc of next small-shell, ch 1, sc in next sc; rep from * around working in corners as follows:

Outer corners: Over the large-shell work ch 1, sk first dc, (sc, ch 2, sc) in next dc, (sc, ch 3, sc) in next dc, (sc, ch 2, sc) in next dc, ch 1, sk last dc.

Inner corners: Work sc2tog over the 2 sc sts at each inner corner.

Join with sl st in first sc. Fasten off.

Weave in ends. •

					26					
				17	27	37				
			10	18	28	38	48			
		5	11	19	29	39	49	59		
	2	6	12	20	30	40	50	60	68	
1	3	7	13	21	31	41	51	61	69	75
	4	8	14	22	32	42	52	62	70	76	80
		9	15	23	33	43	53	63	71	77	81	83
			16	24	34	44	54	64	72	78	82
				25	35	45	55	65	73	79
					36	46	56	66	74	
						47	57	67		
							58			

Granny Square Market Bag

Easy

MEASUREMENTS
Approx 12"/30.5cm square (excluding strap)

MATERIALS
YARN
LION BRAND® Vanna's Choice®, 3½oz/100g balls, each approx 170yd/156m (acrylic)
- 1 ball each in #112 Raspberry (A) and #135 Rust (B)

HOOK
- Size J-10 (6mm) crochet hook, *or size to obtain gauge*

NOTIONS
- Tapestry needle

GAUGE
Rnds 1–4 = approx 5"/12.5cm.
BE SURE TO CHECK YOUR GAUGE.

NOTES
1) Bag is made from two large Granny Squares crocheted together on three sides.
2) To keep Granny Squares even, join new color in a different corner each time the color is changed.
3) After the squares are joined, the Handle is sewn to the top open edge of the Bag and a crocheted edging is worked around top edge of Bag and sides of Handle.

BAG
SQUARE (MAKE 2)
With A, ch 4; join with sl st in first ch to form a ring.
Rnd 1 Ch 3 (counts as dc here and throughout this pattern), 2 dc in ring, ch 2, [3 dc in ring, ch 2] 3 times; join with sl st in top of beg ch.
Rnd 2 With A, ch 4 (counts as dc, ch-1 here and throughout this pattern), *(3 dc, ch 2, 3 dc) in next ch-2 sp (corner made), ch 1; rep from * 2 more times, (3 dc, ch 2, 2 dc) in next corner ch-2 sp; join with sl st in 3rd ch of beg ch-4. Fasten off.
Rnd 3 Join B with sl st in any corner ch-2 sp, ch 3, (2 dc, ch 2, 3 dc) in same ch-2 sp, ch 1, 3 dc in next ch-1 sp, ch 1, *(3 dc, ch 2, 3 dc) in next corner ch-2 sp, ch 1, 3 dc in next ch-1 sp, ch 1; rep from * 2 more times; join with sl st in top of beg ch.
Rnd 4 With B, ch 4, (3 dc, ch 2, 3 dc) in next corner ch-2 sp, ch 1, *(3 dc in next ch-1 sp, ch 1) to next corner ch-2 sp, (3 dc, ch 2, 3 dc) in next corner ch-2 sp, ch 1; rep from * 2 more times, 3 dc in next ch-1 sp, ch 1, 2 dc in last ch-1 sp; join with sl st in 3rd ch of beg ch-4. Fasten off.
Rnd 5 Join A with sl st in any corner ch-2 sp, ch 3, (2 dc, ch 2, 3 dc) in same ch-2 sp, ch 1, (3 dc in next ch-1 sp, ch 1) to next corner ch-2 sp, *(3 dc, ch 2, 3 dc) in next ch-2 sp, ch 1, (3 dc in next ch-1 sp, ch 1) to next corner ch-2 sp; rep from * 2 more times; join with sl st in top of beg ch.
Rnd 6 With A, ch 4, (3 dc, ch 2, 3 dc) in next corner ch-2 sp, ch 1, *(3 dc in next ch-1 sp, ch 1) to next corner ch-2 sp, (3 dc, ch 2, 3 dc) in next corner ch-2 sp, ch 1; rep from * 2 more times, (3 dc in next ch-1 sp, ch 1) to last ch-1 sp, 2 dc in last ch-1 sp; join with sl st in 3rd ch of beg ch-4. Fasten off.
Rnds 7 and 8 With B, rep Rnds 5 and 6.
Rnds 9 and 10 With A, rep Rnds 5 and 6. Fasten off.

HANDLE
With A, ch 73.
Row 1 Sc in 2nd ch from hook, and in each ch across —2 sts.
Rows 2 and 3 Ch 1, turn, sc in each sts across. Fasten off.

FINISHING

Hold Squares with wrong sides together.

Row 1 Working through both Squares, join B with a sl st in any corner ch-2 sp, sc in each sc and ch around 3 sides of Squares, leaving remaining side open for top. Fasten off.

Sew ends of Handle to top of Bag.

TOP EDGING

With right side facing, join B with a sl st anywhere along top edge of Bag.

Rnd 1 Sc evenly spaced across top edge of Bag and along side edge of Handle. Fasten off.

Rep edging on opposite side of Handle and top of Bag.

Weave in ends. •

Vintage Hues Granny Afghan

Easy

SIZE
Approx 37 x 43"/94 x 109cm

MATERIALS
YARN
LION BRAND® Vanna's Choice®, 3½oz/100g balls, each approx 170yd/156m (acrylic) (4)
- 4 balls in #099 Linen (A)
- 2 balls in #101 Pink (B)
- 1 ball each in #105 Silver Blue (C), #108 Dusty Blue (D), #146 Dusty Purple (E), #173 Dusty Green (F), and #125 Taupe (G)

HOOK
- Size J-10 (6mm) crochet hook, *or size to obtain gauge*

NOTIONS
- Tapestry needle

GAUGE
1 Square = approx 6"/15.2cm square.
BE SURE TO CHECK YOUR GAUGE.

NOTES
1) Afghan is made from 42 Squares sewn together following Assembly Diagram.
2) Each Square is worked in joined rounds with Right Side always facing.
3) Edging is worked around the entire outer edge of the assembled Afghan.

BLANKET
SQUARE I (MAKE 12)
With B, ch 4; join with sl st in first ch to form a ring.
Rnd 1 (RS) Ch 3 (counts as first dc on this rnd and on all following rnds), 2 dc in ring, ch 2, [3 dc in ring, ch 2] 3 times; join with sl st in top of beg ch—at the end of this rnd you will have 12 dc and 4 ch-2 sps.

Rnd 2 Ch 3, *dc in each dc to ch-2 sp, (2 dc, ch 2, 2 dc) in ch-2 sp; rep from * around; join with sl st in top of beg ch.

Rnd 3 Rep Rnd 2.
Fasten off B.

Rnd 4 From RS, join A with sl st in any ch-2 sp, ch 3, (dc, ch 2, 2 dc) in same sp, dc in next 2 dc, [ch 1, sk next dc, dc in next dc] 4 times, dc in next dc, *(2 dc, ch 2, 2 dc) in ch-2 sp, dc in next 2 dc, [ch 1, sk next dc, dc in next dc] 4 times, dc in next dc; rep from * 2 more times; join with sl st in top of beg ch.

Rnd 5 Ch 1, sc in same st, sc in next dc, *3 sc in ch-2 sp, sc in each dc and ch-1 sp; rep from * around; join with sl st in top of first sc.
Fasten off A.

SQUARE II (MAKE 9)
Make same as Square I, but work Rnds 1–3 with C and Rnds 4–5 with A.

SQUARE III (MAKE 6)
Make same as Square I, but work Rnds 1–3 with D and Rnds 4–5 with A.

SQUARE IV (MAKE 6)
Make same as Square I, but work Rnds 1–3 with E and Rnds 4–5 with A.

SQUARE V (MAKE 6)
Make same as Square I, but work Rnds 1–3 with F and Rnds 4–5 with A.

Vintage Hues Granny Afghan

SQUARE VI (MAKE 3)
Make same as Square I, but work Rnds 1–3 with G and Rnds 4–5 with A.

FINISHING
Following Assembly Diagram, sew Squares together into 7 strips of 6 squares each. Sew strips together.

EDGING
Rnd 1 From RS, join A with sl st in any sc along outer edge of Afghan, ch 3 (counts as dc), dc in each sc around, working 5 dc in each corner.
Fasten off A.

Rnd 2 From RS, join G with sl st in any dc, ch 1, sc in the same st, sc in each dc around, working 3 sc in each corner.
Fasten off G.

Rnd 3 With A, rep Rnd 1.
Fasten off.

Weave in ends. •

IV	I	IV	I	IV	I
II	III	II	III	II	III
V	I	V	I	V	I
II	VI	II	VI	II	VI
III	I	III	I	III	I
II	V	II	V	II	V
IV	I	IV	I	IV	I